Paleo Diet

Paleo Diet For Beginners Lose Weight, Stay Healthy And
Burn Fat

Healthy Paleo Diet Recipes

David Bailor

Published by David Kruse Publishing House

Paleo Diet: Paleo Diet For Beginners to Lose Weight, Stay Healthy And Burn Fat

(HEALTHY PALEO DIET RECIPES)

ISBN 978-1-989744-16-1

Legal & Disclaimer

TABLE OF CONTENTS

Part -1

Introduction

The paleo craze has taken the world by storm in recent years. You have probably heard a few things about already. However, there's a lot of conflicting information out there that can make it difficult to make a well-informed decision about whether paleo is right for you and how you should go about transitioning into the diet.

Many of the books and websites available will claim to be about paleo but actually contain false or inaccurate information. You'll find paleo recipe books that contain dairy or grains as ingredients (2 of the biggest exclusions from paleo). You'll find websites making misleading claims about what paleo is or is not.

With all this conflicting information, you might find yourself getting overwhelmed at the thought of trying to go paleo. But it's not half so confusing or difficult as it seems. In fact, because it is based on our evolutionary history, it is actually one of the most natural things you could do.

To help you get your footing and get off to a great start with paleo, I have created this comprehensive guide book to help you navigate the world of paleo. In the following chapters, you'll read about:

- What it means to eat and live a paleo lifestyle

- The science behind paleo and why it works

- The most common myths that you'll hear about paleo

- Variations of paleo that you might want to consider doing

- The amazing benefits you'll enjoy by going paleo

- Practical strategies to help you successfully make the transition

- A 30 day meal plan to take all the guesswork out of going paleo

- Absolutely irresistible recipes for all of the meals included in the meal plan (and a few bonus ones just for fun!)

The recipes even include suggested substitutes for any potentially allergenic food meaning you can learn how to easily go paleo even if you've got allergies! So continue reading and get yourself informed and motivated to make the healthy choice of going paleo today!

Chapter 1: What Is Paleo?

The diet was invented back in 1970s but didn't really become widespread until 2002 when the nutrition and exercise specialist, Loren Cordain published a book about paleo. Since then, more and more people have been switching to the diet and realizing just how beneficial it is.

The primary idea behind the diet is to eat a diet similar to what our paleolithic ancestors could have eaten. The reasoning is that much of our modern health problems—diabetes, heart disease, cancer, obesity, etc.—are strongly linked to a poor diet. Most research shows that are ancestors did not suffer from these conditions nearly as often as we do.

Research also shows that many of the foods in our diet that are causing the increased rates of these conditions did not show up in our diet until about 10,000 years ago (when the paleolithic era ended and humans began settling down and farming).

Once farming became widespread, we became more dependent on grains, dairy, and legumes and ate a less varied diet. In the past 100 or so years, things grew worse when food moved from the farm into the factory. We began manufacturing, processing, and chemically altering the foods we ate.

This was done primarily for profit. Fresh produce often had to be sold the same day or within a couple days of being harvested. But foods that were modified to have a longer shelf-life had more time to be sold at the store. Manufacturers started adding more sugar and more salt in an attempt to make their food even more appealing.

All of this led to the modern situation in which you go to the grocery store and see most food sold in packages with long ingredient lists full of chemicals, preservatives, added sugar, added corn syrup, and other things your body has no idea how to digest.

On paleo, you ditch all of these problematic modern foods and return to your roots, so to speak. While there wasn't just one paleo diet—our ancestors at that time had already spread all over the earth and ate different foods depending on their environment—eating a diet rich in whole foods that your ancestors could have accessed through hunting and gathering is a great way to detox your body and nourish it the way it evolved to be nourished.

Separate Myth from Reality

There are lots of myths surrounding paleo that can make it difficult to separate fact from fiction. Unfortunately, some of these myths use pseudoscience to sound like they are true. In this next section, we'll take a look at 5 of the most common myths about eating a paleo diet and break down the reasons why they are wrong.

Paleo Causes Protein Toxicity

Protein toxicity sounds scary, right? And the paleo diet is pretty high in protein compared to other diets. However, this myth falls apart as soon as you do some basic research about protein toxicity.

First of all, in order to be at risk for this condition, you have to have kidney failure or another problem that results in your kidneys not functioning properly. So long as you have healthy kidneys, it's pretty much impossible to eat toxic levels of protein.

You could eat as much as 1 gram of protein per pound of your bodyweight and still not be anywhere near reaching the amount of protein you would need to reach toxic levels for a person with healthy kidneys.

In short: no. Eating a paleo diet will not put you at risk for protein toxicity unless you have a preexisting kidney condition. If you are worried about this, check with your doctor first to assess the health of your kidneys. Otherwise, feel free to enjoy protein rich foods to your heart's content.

Saturated Fat Is Bad for You

For the past 50 or 60 years, most people have been living with the belief that saturated fat leads to heart disease (or that it simply makes you fat). A review of the studies that have been done in these decades show that the links between saturated fat and heart disease simply aren't there.

In most of these studies, those who were categorized as eating a diet high in saturated fats were getting those fats from a typical American diet. That is, they were also eating a lot of sugar, salt, trans fat, and other unhealthy modern ingredients. In studies done on people who eat a *healthy* diet that is high in saturated fats, no increased risk for heart disease was found.

All that is to say, throw away those low-fat diet foods in your fridge and go back to eating full-fat foods. In reality, your body needs fats in order to function. Fat provides energy, nourishes your skin, and protects your digestive system from ulcers and other problems.

The only exception to this rule is trans fat which is a product of the food manufacturing process and not a naturally occurring fat. As long as you avoid processed foods (which you will already be doing on a paleo diet), you can safely avoid this unhealthy form of fat.

Eggs Are Bad for You

Just as saturated fat has gotten a bad rap, so have eggs. For a long time, we have been told to limit the number of eggs we eat because they are high in cholesterol. This is actually true. Eggs are high in cholesterol.

The misunderstanding comes from the failure to differentiate between HDL (good) cholesterol and LDL (bad) cholesterol. Eating foods rich in HDL cholesterol is actually beneficial because it gets into your arteries and veins and actually breaks apart and cleans out all the LDL cholesterol that is clogging your arteries. That is, if you have a cholesterol problem, you want to start eating more foods rich in HDL cholesterol to help manage the problem. You'll also want to eat more fiber but that's a different story.

The point is, yes, eggs are high in cholesterol but they are high in HDL (good) cholesterol which means they will ultimately help you lower your LDL (bad) cholesterol. With that said, there is absolutely no reason to moderate the amount of eggs you eat. Eat to your heart's content—because the LDL cholesterol lowering power of eggs will literally make your heart content!

Going Paleo Is Expensive

The next most common myth regarding paleo is the idea that eating this diet is simply too expensive. First of all, the cost of food will very much depend on where you live and how much certain foods cost in that area.

Secondly, if you budget right, you and your family can eat a nutritious paleo diet without spending an extra dime. Yes, fresh meats and produce (the staples of paleo) do cost more than processed junk food in most cases.

However, you can buy in bulk and buy directly from farms to cut down on costs. You can also buy frozen and canned versions of food if necessary (so long as nothing has been added in the process of freezing or canning). You can also look to cut costs in other areas of your budget to free up more cash for groceries.

For example, practice better energy efficiency at home in order to lower your utilities bill and use the money saved there to splurge on quality ingredients to nourish your body with.

If that isn't enough to dispel the myth that paleo is too expensive, consider the money you will be saving by getting healthy. When you nourish your body consistently, you will get sick less often and be less prone to injury. That means you will be spending a lot less on medical bills.

So even if you end up spending a little bit more at the grocery store, you'll be spending a whole lot less at the hospital!

Fasting Is Required

In some versions of paleo, this is true. They do advocate fasting on occasion. The theory here is that occasional short term fasting (usually about 1 day) will boost your metabolism.

The science here is a bit shaky, though, so there's not much to really prove whether or not short term fasting actually does anything to help your metabolism. However, doing a 1 day fast every few months is likely not serious enough to cause any long term damage to your body.

So, basically, it comes down to your own plans. If you want to fast for one day once every couple of months, you can. But this is, by no means, a strict requirement of the traditional paleo diet.

With these common myths dispelled and the history of how the current paleo diet was developed, you now have the background information you need to start learning more about the day to day requirements of the paleo lifestyle.

In the next chapter, you'll learn more about the specifics of what you should and shouldn't eat. You'll also get some information about the different variations of paleo that have come out since it was first developed back in the 70s.

Chapter 2: Living the Paleo Lifestyle

Most people refer to paleo as a diet but it's more accurate to refer to it as a lifestyle. There are a few reasons for this. First of all, the full paleo diet actually also includes recommendations for exercise and physical activity that should be done along with eating paleo food.

More importantly, the word "diet" tends to imply something temporary that you do just to lose weight before switching back to your normal eating habits. In order to see the best results with paleo, you shouldn't treat it as a diet. Treat it as your new way of life.

In this chapter, we'll take a closer look at what you should and shouldn't eat on paleo. Then, we'll talk briefly about some of the variations of paleo that have popped over the past decade. Finally, we'll dive into the paleo philosophy on exercise. Don't cringe at that word—you might be pleasantly surprised!

What You Should Eat

Here are the main foods you should focus on eating to live a healthy, balanced paleo lifestyle:

Meat

In the original diet, it is recommended that you get about 50% of your calories from animal protein (this includes fish discussed below). This might sound like a lot especially if you've been living under the impression that meat isn't really that good for you.

However, it's important to know that some of our paleolithic era ancestors—namely, the ones living further up north with minimal access to plant foods—ate a diet that was very near 100% meat. Of course, that was out of necessity rather than health reasons. The point is, humans can and do thrive on a meat-heavy diet.

In no way does paleo advocate mimicking this extreme northern diet of almost exclusively meat. But you can still get 50% of your calories from meat and get plenty of other nutritious foods in your diet as well. The key to a healthy paleo diet is balance and variety.

Meat provides one of the best sources of protein that our body can readily absorb and use. In terms of nutrient density, meat provides more protein with fewer calories than other protein sources (like grains or legumes which you'll be giving up for paleo).

Many of the seemingly unhealthy aspects of meat are either untrue or misunderstood. For example, you just read about saturated fat in the previous chapter and why it's actually an important part of your diet. But meat is also high in unsaturated fats which are equally important.

The cholesterol issue is another poorly understood topic. Red meat has long been demonized as a cholesterol raising food just like eggs. But, as you read in the previous chapter, there's a difference between good (HDL) cholesterol and bad (LDL) cholesterol.

To sum up that section of the previous quickly: you *want* to raise your healthy HDL cholesterol levels because this will naturally lower your unhealthy LDL cholesterol. Good HDL cholesterol comes from healthy unsaturated fats. While meat does have some, the best sources of unsaturated fats are plant oils (olive, almond, etc.) and fish.

If you eat enough of these HDL cholesterol foods, you'll keep your cholesterol levels perfectly balanced without effort or concern (provided you don't have a preexisting health condition).

In a balanced diet, red meat can't do any damage because:

a) You are eating lots of healthy unsaturated fats that keep your HDL cholesterol high (and, therefore, your LDL cholesterol low).

b) The overwhelming majority of bad LDL cholesterol is actually produced by our own body as a reaction to stress or inflammation. In reality, we absorb very little LDL cholesterol from food.

So, to sum it all up: eat lots of meat *and* eat lots of fresh fruits and vegetables and other paleo foods as well. Think of meat as that friend that's really fun in a crowd but not so much when it's just the two of you. The "crowd" in this case refers to all the fresh produce that should be on your plate alongside the meat.

Fish

For some people, fish is really obviously a category of meat. For others, it's so obviously *not* a meat that people could still call themselves "vegetarian" even if they still eat fish. Whatever side of the debate you land on, you should be eating lots of it.

The reason it's given its own separate section from meat in this chapter is because the health benefits it provides differ from other meats in a few key ways.

First of all, the main type of fat found in fish is *unsaturated* fat rather than saturated fat. That is, it's one of those powerful HDL cholesterol raising foods. Much of this fat comes in the form of omega-3 fatty acids which strengthen the heart and brain while giving you amazing skin.

Aside from the amazing power of fish fat, it's also extremely nutrient dense while being relatively low in calories at the same time.

In short, including a whole lot more fish in your diet is one of the best decisions you could make. Eat it every day if you can. If not, try to eat it at least 3 times per week. In the 30 day meal plan you'll get in chapter 5, you'll see that fish (or seafood more generally) is part of around 4-5 meals each week.

Fruits

Fruits are nature's dessert. They are delicious and so richly flavorful. They also happen to be super healthy. If you've got a serious sweet tooth, the natural fruit sugars will help combat it without having to resort to foods with refined white sugar.

If you've been eating a lot of sugary processed foods until now, be prepared for an adjustment period. Fruits won't taste nearly sweet enough in comparison because you have become so accustomed to a sugar overdose. However, after the first couple of weeks, you will notice that fruit becomes sweeter and sweeter with every bite. This is because your body is learning to recognize normal levels of sweetness again.

In the world of fruits, there are so many amazing varieties that each provide their own benefits. Most berries, for example, are extremely rich sources of antioxidants—the buzzword vitamins that help protect your cells from damage and fight cancer. Bananas are world famous for their potassium—the mineral that lowers blood pressure and strengthens your bones and muscles.

Eating a wide variety of fruits will provide you with a full range of vitamins and minerals. But keep in mind: eating fruits means actually eating them. Don't become tempted by fruit juices. Even if there is no added sugar and the bottle brands itself as healthy, juice is simply not a healthy way to consume fruit.

The reason juice is unhealthy is because it squeezes out all the sugary liquid in fruit and leaves the fibrous flesh behind. Since you aren't going to be eating grains or legumes on your paleo diet, it's important that you get all the fiber you need from fruits and vegetables.

The fiber in the flesh of the fruit also helps regulate the digestion of the fruit sugars so that you don't end up with a huge spike in blood sugar—which will raise blood pressure and lead to a killer crash that will cause serious sugar cravings.

The bottom line when it comes to fruit: eat a wide variety of whole fruits (not juice!) to provide your body with a good source of fiber and all the essential vitamins and minerals.

Vegetables

Vegetables are the other side of the coin. Together with fruits, they will provide you with fiber, vitamins, and minerals. Since they are low in sugar compared to fruits, they are actually the healthier of the two. However, that's not a criticism against fruit so much as further motivation to eat a whole lot of vegetables as well.

Many people have a tough time eating enough vegetables. In fact, most Americans (around 80%) eat far less vegetables than they should.

Approximately 20% eat don't eat any vegetables at all!

The standard recommendation for fruit and vegetable consumption is to eat 9 servings per day. Now, you might very understandably be asking: what on earth is a "serving"? This is the main problem with that standard recommendation. To make it a lot easier, let's translate it into an actual measurement of food:

To meet your 9 serving minimum, you need to eat 2 cups of fruit and 2 ½ cups of vegetables.

Now, that's actually not that much. Some of the smoothie recipes you'll find in chapter 9 include contain at least that much fruits and veggies. Of course, this 2 cups + 2 ½ cups is a *minimum*. You can (and should) eat more than that. Just use this measure as a baseline to make sure that you are including enough fruits and veggies in your day.

Eggs

Eggs are a staple of every paleo diet variation (at least all of the ones discussed later on in this chapter). In fact, eggs are so standard for paleo that some people quickly become sick of them. For that reason, the recipes found in chapters 6 through 9 try to keep the egg-heavy recipes to a reasonable level to help you avoid getting tired of them.

Egg exhaustion aside, these little guys are actually one of the most nutritious foods you can eat. Hence why paleo includes so many. Think about it: inside that little shell are all the nutrients needed to create a whole living creature (a chicken).

The yolk has a full range of vitamins and minerals. It's also got a lot of protein and healthy fats. It packs a lot of cholesterol but, as you already read, that's mostly healthy HDL cholesterol so they actually help you combat the bad LDL cholesterol.

Because of this, eggs are a great way to round out any meal. If you're in need of a nutritious and quick protein to add to your dish, just crack an egg or two over it!

You already learned a bit about eggs in the previous chapter so we won't go into too much more detail here. The bottom line is: eat eggs. Eat as many eggs as your heart desires. If you're not a huge fan of eggs, make an effort to change your tastes and start appreciating them.

Nuts & Seeds

Like eggs, nuts and seeds are another great source of quick protein to help round out just about any meal. They are also rich in nearly every vitamin and mineral you need. You can think of them as the "eggs" of the plant world since they are both the compact package of all the nutrients needed to produce a living thing. In the case of nuts and seeds, they have what's needed to grow an entire tree (or other plant).

Nuts are a fantastic source of unsaturated fats. Between the fats, antioxidants, and vitamin E, they are also one of the best foods to eat to improve your skin.

On paleo, they are a staple alternative to grains. When ground into a flour or meal, they can be used in much the same way you would use grain flour. When roasted, they can be used to make a healthy paleo granola.

They are also perfect for between meal snacks. In chapter 9, you'll get a recipe for paleo granola and energy bars—both of which contain nuts as their primary ingredients.

Herbs & Spices

We all know herbs and spices are some of the best sources of flavor in meals. Food would just be that much less exciting if we couldn't add a kick of cayenne or sprinkle of cinnamon.

However, herbs and spices don't just add flavor. They also add nutrients. As plants—albeit usually ground up into a fine powder—they provide many of the same vitamins and minerals that vegetables do.

If you don't consider yourself much of cook and aren't sure how to season food, don't worry. Just start experimenting. If you're not sure a particular seasoning will work in the dish you are preparing, smell it. Does the smell of that spice seem to blend well with the smell of your dish? If so, add a dash.

If not, add a dash anyway. Sometimes, contrasting flavors come together well in a dish.

Just start with a dash to see how it works. If it doesn't work, you've learned your lesson—it might not taste as good but it's not going to kill you to eat it. On the other hand, if it does work, you've just discovered a new flavor combination all on your own!

Liberal experimentation with herbs and spices is the best way to keep your paleo diet fun and exciting. It's also the best way to push your cooking skills to the limit and actually become something of a chef in the kitchen.

No matter what your current cooking experience is, experimenting in the kitchen will help you improve. The more skilled you become with cooking, the more delicious your healthy meals will become.

Oils & Fats

On paleo, you won't be able to eat butter. But, as hard as it might be to believe now, you'll hardly miss it. That's because you can eat lots of other sources of fat including (but not limited to):

Olive Oil

Coconut Oil

Lard

Ghee (a clarified butter which is often considered paleo-friendly although not technically strict paleo)

These can each be used as butter substitutes in any recipe you enjoy that calls for butter. They are healthier options because they are more readily digested by your body than butter is.

A quick note here: you cannot eat margarine as a butter substitute. This is a heavily processed food that usually contains a lot of Trans fats.

Olive oil is an amazing source of unsaturated fats and should be drizzled over just about everything you eat. Coconut oil provides healthy saturated fats and a rich flavor to your food. Lard gives you that rich, full-bodied animal fat flavor that you might be missing without butter. It's also the best option in recipes that call for a solidified form of fat.

It is recommended to get about 20% to 25% of your calories from healthy (unsaturated and saturated) fats. Now, this doesn't mean you should start downing glasses of oil. Remember, you also get these healthy fats from fish, nuts, seeds, and some plant foods (especially avocados).

You don't want to get all your healthy fats from one source. Eat a wide variety of different sources. But definitely include liberal helpings of these healthy oils and fats in that variety!

What You Shouldn't Eat

Now that we've covered all the delicious foods you should be eating, let's take a brief look at the foods you'll need to cut out (or at least seriously minimize):

Sugar

Refined sugar is one of the worst things you can put in your body. While most people assume that fat makes you fat (a false assumption that we have already talked about in chapter 1), it's actually more accurate to say that sugar makes you fat.

This is because refined sugar doesn't get absorbed at a steady rate. It is already so broken down that your body can immediately absorb all of it at once. This is why drinking a can of soda leads to an immediate spike in energy levels. But it's also why you feel a severe energy crash shortly after.

Our paleo ancestors did not have the technology to produce refined sugar. The only sugar they ate came from whole food sources—the most significant source being fruit.

The sugar found in fructose is not as refined as that found in soda and other processed foods. It still breaks down quickly compared to other forms of energy (fiber, protein, and fat). However, fruits often also contain fiber, fat, or even protein.

The complex structure of the fruit helps to regulate the rate at which you absorb its sugar. This is why eating a whole fruit is far healthier than drinking juice.

By giving up sugar, you will see the following benefits:

Lower blood pressure: with stabilized blood sugar levels, you won't be placing excess strain on your body to deal with the sugar overload. This will help normalize your blood pressure.

Weight loss: again by stabilizing your blood sugar levels, you allow your body to process energy from food at a steady rate. This means it has the time to use the "fuel" from the food you eat throughout the day. With sugar, all that "fuel" comes in one large dose. All the excess that you can't use immediately gets stored as fat. So, by cutting out sugar, you will decrease the amount of calories that end up getting stored as fat.

More alert: with the energy spikes from sugar, it becomes hard to focus on any one task. The energy crashes that follow make you feel foggy and fatigued. By stabilizing your energy levels, you'll be able to maintain a consistent level of alertness and focus throughout the day.

Lower cholesterol: a dangerous amount of the fat that you store from sugar gets deposited into the liver. Your liver than eliminates this by sending it out into the blood stream in the form of LDL (bad) cholesterol. By giving up sugar, your body will start naturally producing less LDL cholesterol.

Lower risk of heart disease: with the lower cholesterol and lower blood pressure, you are keeping your heart free from stress and strain. It will be able to stay strong and healthy naturally.

Lower risk of obesity: as you already read, cutting out sugar helps you lose weight. The most important health factor about this weight loss is that it helps you lose belly fat and visceral fat. Visceral fat is the fat stored in your organs (like your liver). This is the most dangerous fat because it can interrupt the functioning of your organs. Belly fat is a huge risk factor for visceral fat. By cutting out sugar, you will get rid of these dangerous forms of fat.

Increased appetite control: there is yet another way that eating sugar makes you fat. It decreases your sensitivity to a hormone called leptin. Leptin's job is to tell your body when you feel full. By decreasing your sensitivity to leptin, then, sugar is preventing you from feeling full. This keeps you eating and eating even when your body doesn't actually want anything. When you cut sugar, you will immediately notice that you feel more satisfied after meals and stay fuller for longer between meals.

Improved skin: sugar accelerates the ageing process by making collagen less supple and decreasing the elasticity of our skin. By simply cutting out sugar, you can not only slow down but actually reverse the wrinkling and sagging of your skin. You will notice your skin become softer, smoother, and more radiant.

Reduced pain: sugar causes inflammation and irritation all throughout your body. It weakens just about every structure in your body, putting them at higher risk for damage. When you cut sugar out, then, you will reduce inflammation and strengthen every single cell in your body so that you are at a lower risk for injury and experience less pain overall.

Processed Foods

The main reason processed foods need to be cut from your diet is because they either contain refined sugar or Trans fats (or both). Since we have already discussed sugar in detail above, we'll focus on Trans fat here.

Trans fat is a kind of fat that is produced when manufacturers add hydrogen to liquid fat in order to make them more solid. On ingredient lists, Trans fats appear as "hydrogenated fats" or "partially hydrogenated fats."

Food manufacturers do this because hydrogenated fats are cheaper to produce than naturally solid fats like butter or lard. Studies have shown that they raise LDL (bad) cholesterol and lower your HDL (good) cholesterol at the same time.

This has disastrous effects on your health. Not only is it adding LDL cholesterol but it's removing the HDL cholesterol that would otherwise be helping you to get rid of the excess bad cholesterol.

In addition to raising your bad cholesterol to dangerous levels, Trans fats also increase your risk for diabetes by as much as 40%. The reasons for this are not yet completely clear but early studies suggest that it might be because Trans fats decrease your sensitivity to insulin.

Trans fats are so bad, in fact, that most countries (except for the United States) have actually banned them altogether.

By giving up processed foods which often contain near-toxic levels of Trans fats, sugar, and salt, you'll notice the following benefits:

Decreased inflammation: both sugar and Trans fats lead to inflammation of joints, arteries, and organs. So, by cutting them out, you can reduce your risk for heart disease, diabetes, and arthritis. If you already have any of these conditions, cutting out processed foods will help you manage them and decrease the painful symptoms.

Improved circulation: not only do processed foods cause your body to produce more LDL cholesterol, it also hardens your arteries and veins. This means your arteries and clogged and unable to dilate at the same time. When you give up processed foods, then, the LDL cholesterol will clear up and your arteries will be stronger and more flexible. This will improve circulation which will have many fantastic effects on your mood, energy levels, and overall physical health.

Lower risk for muscle damage: with improved circulation, your body can now deliver more oxygen and nutrients to your muscles. As you become more active, this will become important. If you've ever gone for a run or tried to lift weights only to feel a burning pain in your muscles, this is because they do not have enough oxygen. With better circulation, your muscles will be able to endure much more activity without feeling that burning pain.

Improved metabolism: without processed foods, your digestion will quickly improve. You won't retain as much water weight. You'll be more sensitive to insulin, you'll have more regular bowel movements which means less bloating and a lower risk for colon cancer.

Weight loss: after giving up processed foods, your body will quickly start to work on burning up any dangerous visceral fat and belly fat that is stored in your body. You'll also become more sensitive to leptin which is the hormone responsible for making you feel full. These facts together with the improved metabolism will lead to rapid healthy weight loss. If you add in more light activities throughout the week, the results will be even more amazing.

Grains

Grains have only been in the human diet for about 10,000 years. Our paleolithic ancestors did consume them on rare occasions but the wild versions were not so easy to use. They were smaller and much more difficult to harvest.

Once we learned how to grow them ourselves, we quickly started to produce grains that were larger and easier to harvest. They soon became one of the easiest foods to access as well as store for long winters. This meant that grains took the center stage in our diet very quickly.

While they did help us avoid starvation, the speed with which we switched from hardly ever eating grains to eating an almost exclusively grain diet caused some problems for our digestion. Our bodies have still not had the time to evolve and adapt to the high amount of grains that are found in the modern diet.

The main challenge that grains present to our digestion is gluten. In some people, celiac disease means they cannot tolerate any gluten at all. This is a very small group of people, though. More commonly, you'll find people with gluten sensitivity. This shares many symptoms with lactose intolerance but it also causes chronic fatigue, headaches, and other problems.

Even if you don't have celiac disease or gluten sensitivity, your body still has a tough time dealing with gluten. In recent studies done on people who have neither of these conditions, there were still many negative effects resulting from a gluten diet.

A high gluten diet in otherwise healthy individuals lead to more bloating, more pain, and fatigue. It also led to inflammation of the intestines and broke down the lining of the intestines (putting them at risk for ulcers and other painful conditions).

In some cases, it can cause irritable bowel syndrome (IBS). In those who already had irritable bowel syndrome, gluten was found to make the condition worse.

If you still can't imagine living without grains even after reading through all of these terrible health effects, you might consider opting for gluten-free grains. In the modern paleo variation which you'll read about below, gluten-free grains like quinoa, brown rice, and oats are perfectly acceptable.

However, it's best to go totally grain free for at least the first 30 days just to give yourself a chance to see how your body feels after giving up these harmful foods.

Without gluten, you'll soon notice the following benefits:

Improved energy levels: even in otherwise healthy individuals, gluten often causes chronic fatigue. In severe cases, people will sleep for as much as 15 hours in the day. Once you eliminate gluten, you'll notice that you sleep better and that you probably require less sleep than you might have thought. You'll feel more rested when you wake up and avoid mid-afternoon crashes.

Improved appetite control: with better sleep and improved energy levels, you'll be able to avoid those tough cravings that usually occur when your energy levels start to drop. You can fight off temptations more easily and avoid feeling like you need to eat even when you aren't hungry.

Improved mood: with a healthier digestive system, you'll have stabilized blood sugar levels and improved circulation. Both of these will help your mood by preventing low-energy crankiness and stabilizing the hormones that trigger other negative emotions like stress, anxiety, and sadness. Of course, this doesn't mean you'll never feel sad again. Emotions aren't entirely controlled by your body. However, you will have a much easier time managing your emotions and avoiding unexplained mood swings.

Improved skin: with a strong digestive system, you'll notice clear, healthier skin as well. This is because your digestive system is your first line of defense against toxins. With a better functioning digestive system, you'll be able to clear out toxins before they leak into your body and wreak havoc. This will improve all organs but, since you can't see the other ones, you will only notice the improvement in your skin. Wrinkles will disappear and your skin will become more smooth and elastic.

Dairy

Like grains, dairy has only very recently made an appearance in our diet. While there were some nomadic groups that drank milk when there was no access to water, the majority of humans didn't start drinking animal milk until they settled down and began farming.

In these early times, drinking animal milk was done out of necessity. Without regular access to clean drinking water, milk was the only way to stave off dehydration. Eventually, the milk-drinking populations adapted to be able to digest lactose (milk sugar) well into adulthood.

Before this time, humans only had the ability to digest milk as infants when they drank their mother's milk. Once they were weaned, they would lose this ability to digest milk. Today, around 65% of all humans on earth are still unable to digest milk after infancy. That means the majority of people are "lactose intolerant."

Even in those who are tolerant, lactose—like gluten—is still difficult to digest. This is the main reason for eliminating dairy in a paleo diet. You will likely have improved digestion function after giving it up.

Like grains, however, this is one of the foods that is sometimes allowed in certain variations of paleo. However, rather than drinking milk which contains a high amount of lactose, it is recommended to stick to cheese, yogurt and other dairy products made from the milk.

This is because, in the process of making these dairy products, the lactose in the milk is broken down into a form that is easier on the digestive system. In either case, try to stay dairy free for at least the first 30 days. Then, if you find you still miss your cheese and yogurt, slowly reintroduce it to see if your body really can tolerate it.

Legumes

Legumes were scarce prior to the advent of farming. They were difficult to gather and use in the paleolithic era. But, with farming, it became easier to grow and consume them.

While they are traditionally considered to be a very healthy food, they are actually a little bit deceiving. Yes, legumes often contain a lot of fiber, protein, vitamins, and minerals. However, what few people know is that they also contain something known as phytic acid.

Phytic acid is also sometimes referred to as an anti-nutrient. This is because when it gets into your system, it prevents your body from absorbing the other nutrients in the food you ate. This means that the high nutrient content found in legumes is more or less going to waste since the phytic acid they also contain will prevent you from absorbing it.

Research has shown that this phytic acid is broken down and destroyed in the cooking process which means that there may be some good news for bean lovers. As long as you thoroughly cook your beans, you should be able to destroy at least the majority of the phytic acid.

However, as with grains and dairy, make sure to commit to at least 30 days without them. After 30 days of strict paleo, you can slowly reintroduce these foods to see how your body reacts to them. The only two that you should never reintroduce again are sugar and processed foods.

Most Alcohol

Nearly every version of paleo will recommend giving up alcohol. However, most do allow for red wine in moderate amounts. Moderate in this case means no more than 1-2 glasses per day.

Beer is absolutely off limits since it is made from grains. The gluten in beer will have the same harmful effects that were discussed earlier in the section about grains.

Most hard liquors are also made from grains or carbohydrate-rich starchy foods. Red wine is one of the few alcohols that are grain free and do not contain added sugar. Even with that, however, you have to be careful. Many of the low quality wines available do contain added sugar in order to mask the bad taste.

So if you are going to be drinking red wine, make sure you splurge on a quality bottle. Do your background research to find wines that are produced without added sugar. Stick to these brands that you know are safe.

While this will mean you spend a little more on each bottle, you will save money in the long run by moderating the amount you drink.

Beyond the issues of gluten and sugar, alcohol is also counterproductive if you are trying to lose weight. When you drink an alcoholic beverage, you launch a whole series of processes that lead to weight gain. Let's break down that process.

First, you are consuming a sugary, high calorie beverage. Yes, the sugar is technically natural but, just like fruit juice, you aren't consuming the fibrous flesh of the fruit which acts as a natural regulator to make sure you don't absorb the sugar too quickly.

Secondly, you redirect your metabolism. When your body has to deal with alcohol, it goes into a sort of panic. It is unable to store alcohol as fat so it has to burn through all of it immediately. In order to make sure it does this, it completely stops burning through any fat, sugar, or other calories in your body and focuses only on burning up the alcohol.

This means that so long as there is alcohol in your system, you are not actually burning any calories (except for the alcohol calories). Instead, your body immediately stores everything else as fat because it knows it can do that with everything else except the alcohol.

This is where that "beer belly" comes from. Regular consumption of alcohol keeps your body in a constant state of burning alcohol for energy and storing everything else you consume as fat.

When you feel hungover in the morning, this is also a result of your body attempting to burn through the rest of the alcohol that is still in your system.

In addition to stopping the fat burning process altogether, alcohol also dehydrates. On average, you lose about 1.5x as much water as the amount of alcohol you drank.

This rapid loss of water leads to dehydration which also leads to weight gain. You can think of water as oil in your car. Without oil, the gears grind together, heat up, and eventually become irreparably damaged. Without water, similar things will occur in your body.

Your metabolism will slow as solids have a difficult time moving through your system without liquid. Your circulation will slow down as your blood becomes thicker and less fluidic. Your body will become stressed and produce cortisol, a hormone which tells your body to start storing more fat.

The bottom line is, if you are trying to lose a lot of weight, you should give up alcohol altogether—including red wine. However, if you are more interested in maintaining your weight (or just losing a few pounds), you can continue to drink red wine in moderation.

Once you have your weight under control, red wine can actually be a healthy part of your diet when consumed in moderation. Fermented fruit juices (like wine) have been a part of the human diet for a long time. They often contain lots of probiotics and antioxidants which are both essential for a healthy body.

Paleo Diet Variations

There are as many variations of paleo as there are people on this diet. Here are a few of the more common ones:

Modern Paleo

Modern paleo excludes processed and manufactured foods and grains that contain gluten. However, unlike the traditional version, you can eat gluten-free whole grains (quinoa, brown rice, etc.) and dairy so long as your body doesn't have an adverse reaction to them.

The logic behind this is that our bodies have, indeed, started to evolve and adapt to modern foods so we don't need to be strictly paleo. However, there are still many of us whose bodies are not adapted to gluten (celiac disease or gluten sensitivity) or the lactose in dairy products (lactose intolerance). For those people, it's best to eat a stricter version that excludes those foods your body can't process.

You still need to avoid processed foods, sugar, and legumes and even if you eat both grains and dairy, it should be in moderation and they should be high quality.

Organic Paleo

Organic paleo follows the same exact guidelines as the normal paleo diet. The difference here is that there is a greater emphasis on the importance of eating purely organic foods.

All beef and pork should be grass-fed, eggs should be free range, and all produce should be organically grown. This is, for obvious reasons, more expensive but worth it if you've got the cash to do it. Organic foods are often more nutrient dense and more richly flavorful than nonorganic.

Vegetarian Paleo

This variation is exactly what its name implies. Its paleo without the meat. You can choose whether or not to include fish (some consider it to still be vegetarian). Because of the lack of meat, there is an increased emphasis on eggs, nuts, and seeds to make sure the protein requirements are being met.

Low Fructose Paleo

This variation of paleo takes a stricter stance against sugar by including the natural fructose found in fruits in that category. That is, it emphasizes eating fruits in moderation and focusing on the other foods allowed in paleo (meat, fish, vegetables, etc.). It also usually emphasizes getting rid of honey and maple syrup as well.

This doesn't mean you need to have an all-out ban on fruits. You can certainly still eat them but the majority of your produce sources should be vegetables.

Whole 30 Paleo

On the whole 30 version, you eat a strict paleo diet without any cheating for 30 straight days. Afterwards, you can decide to stick with it or gradually reintroduce grains and dairy for a modern paleo diet.

The idea here is that you need to give your body a chance to figure out if it can actually tolerate these foods. Some people are lactose intolerant or gluten insensitive without ever realizing it. They feel pain or discomfort on a regular basis and are never sure why. By doing strict paleo for 30 straight days, you give your body a chance to detox and see if the change makes you feel better.

If you choose to reintroduce grains and dairy, do so one at a time. Give yourself at least 2 weeks to see if you are feeling any discomfort after reintroducing each one.

Intermittent Fasting Paleo

This is not so much a variation of paleo as another guideline that can be added to any of the variations you choose. This guideline emphasizes fasting for a 24 hour period once in a while. The time frame can differ but it's usually either once every 2 weeks or once per month.

The proposed benefit is that short-duration fasting helps boost your metabolism. There's not a lot of science to support this but that's partly because there are just not a lot of studies that have been done on short-duration fasting so it's hard to say if it helps or not.

If you are otherwise in good health, you can try it safely to see if it works for you. However, if you have any conditions like diabetes, hypoglycemia, or other troubles with blood sugar regulation, I would highly recommend you avoid fasting for any amount of time.

Slow Carb Paleo

This variation is somewhat similar to modern paleo except that it still excludes dairy. The only change from the normal paleo diet is that you can eat whole grains (including those with gluten). However, you don't eat them regularly. Instead, you alternate between higher carb and lower carb periods (usually lasting 1-2 weeks).

Beyond the Kitchen

Now that you know the ins and outs of how to eat on a paleo diet—whichever variation you choose—it's time to turn to the rest of the lifestyle.

Exercising on Paleo

Exercise is, indeed, recommended on paleo. However, the approach is somewhat unique. Doing intense workouts is only recommended about 3-4 times per week maximum.

It's considered more important to focus on becoming more active overall rather than just including an intense workout routine and then just sitting around the rest of the day.

Our ancestors did not work out for 1 hour and then just sit behind a desk or on the couch the rest of the time. They did moderate low intensity exercise most of the day with occasional bursts of high intensity when it was necessary—such as to chase an animal they were hunting or to run away from a predator who was hunting them.

When you do high intensity exercise, focus on strength but incorporate a little cardio. Throughout the rest of your day, focus on light cardio.

The Paleo Lifestyle

To get a lot of moderate exercise into your day, you need to change your lifestyle so that you are more physically active. This can take some creativity and rearranging but it is possible and you will be thankful you made this change after you've done it.

As it is, you probably spend your days in an office and then come home to sit on a couch in front of the TV. You walk around minimally and you drive to work. Most of this probably seems like a necessity—as if there wasn't another way to do what you need to do or relax after a hard day's work.

If that's your mindset, it's high time you change your mentality. Here are a few tips for including more physical activity into your daily lifestyle:

Cut down on television

Breaking the TV habit might seem hard but it will only take a few days before you realize that you hardly even miss it. You don't have to give it up altogether but cut it down to no more than 30 to 60 minutes per day. You should be able to go an entire day without ever turning on the TV.

Use all the time you are saving from not watching TV to get active with your family. Go for a walk or a bike ride with the family. Get out of the house and play a sport with friends.

Take post-meal walks

After each meal you eat, take a short 15-20 minute walk. Just take it easy and enjoy some fresh air while you help get the blood pumping and activate your metabolism. A few short walks throughout the day will add up quickly and it's a great way to lower stress—which also happens to boost your metabolism!

Walk and talk

Even when you're really busy and feel like you've got an insurmountable pile of work on your hands, you can still find ways to work in some physical activity.

For example, suggest holding "on the go" meetings where you and your coworkers take a walk around the block or to a nearby park and discuss business while walking.

If you've got a lot of phone calls to make, you aren't attached to your desk. Get the list of contacts and go for a walk while you work your way through it.

If you're trying to work out a problem or obstacle to a current project, walk while you think. The increased blood flow will actually help you brainstorm more effectively.

Bike to work

Biking to work is a great way to make sure you get some physical activity at least twice per day (once on the way there and once on the way back). It also helps lower stress and keep you out of the morning and evening traffic jams.

If you commute out of town to work, consider taking a train or bus. Then, bike to and from the station each day. During your commute on the train or bus, you'll have extra time to relax, read, or catch up on emails for work. That's way better than just sitting in traffic and stressing about the time!

Go on weekend adventures

Unlike during the work week, your days off are yours to make the most of. Use your weekends to take short trips. Go hiking in some nearby mountains or hills. Take up rock climbing. Sign up for a dance class. Go toss the Frisbee around in the park with your dog.

Get outside and get your body moving as much as possible on the weekend. But don't let it feel like a workout. The point of paleo is not to be miserable. Do activities that you enjoy and do them often.

If you're not a very active person now and aren't sure what you enjoy, don't worry. Just start by trying out a lot of different activities until you land on one that speaks to you.

Chapter 3: The Science behind Why Paleo Works

The entire paleo logic is based on the idea that our bodies have not yet evolved to deal with the modern diet. From an evolutionary perspective, our digestive systems and nutrient requirements are still "stuck" back in the paleolithic era.

In some ways this is, indeed, true. However, it often gets a little oversimplified by some which can lead to heated debates that totally miss the point of paleo. For example, people argue that paleo is flawed because not everyone in the paleolithic era ate the same diet.

It's true that there were varied diets depending on the region our ancestors lived in. However, the point is to eat foods that were *available* at that time, not to perfectly mimic a specific regional diet.

The focus here is on eating natural, unprocessed whole foods that didn't result from modern developments like agriculture or food manufacturing. With that in mind, let's take a look at why paleo can have the amazing benefits that it does.

The Diet

As soon as you eliminate processed foods and sugar, you are going to notice a difference. To understand why you start feeling and looking so much better after giving up these two things, let's take a look at what they are doing in your body.

Whenever you eat any food, your body immediately starts to break it down. Even when it enters your mouth, your saliva is already working to break down the food.

So when you down a can of soda, for example, your body will break it down immediately. This is because the sugar it contains is already extremely refined. The manufacturing process has basically "digested" it for you. That means by the time it reaches your stomach, all that sugar will get absorbed immediately into your blood stream. The entire dosage of sugar enters your blood stream almost immediately.

Compare this to meat. Meat is a complex food that takes a long time to breakdown and use. So, rather than getting all of the energy from it at once, it reaches your blood stream little by little.

With sugary processed foods, you often consume enough sugar to energize you for the whole day but you absorb it all at once. This puts your body in an immediate surplus. All the excess sugar that it doesn't need right then will be converted and stored as fat.

When you eat healthy whole foods that take more time to break down, you use more of it and store less of it as fat because it's not getting absorbed all in one large dose.

What this means for you is:

More stable energy levels (no more spikes and crashes)

Weight loss (particularly in the belly)

Lower blood pressure

The next food group that is restricted on most variations of paleo is grains. Most grains contain gluten. This is a starchy substance that can cause digestion problems in a lot of people. For those with celiac disease, gluten causes sever health issues.

There are also people with gluten sensitivity. This is less severe than celiac disease but it does still cause problems. Some of the symptoms of gluten sensitivity include bloating, abdominal pain, joint pain, chronic fatigue, headaches, and irritable bowels.

For many people, giving up gluten leads to better digestion, less inflammation of the joints and arteries, and a more energized or alert mood.

Dairy is another recent addition to the human diet. As mammals, we have long been able to digest milk as infants. But the ability to digest lactose (the sugar found in milk) usually disappears shortly after we are weaned.

Humans began drinking the milk of other animals out of necessity. For people without access to clean drinking water, the milk from the animals they kept was the only safe way to stay hydrated.

Today, some people have developed "lactose persistence." That is, the ability to digest milk even after being weaned. In reality, the ability to digest milk is actually the exception to the rule. The overwhelming majority of people in the world are lactose intolerance.

Even for those who can still digest lactose, it can still be rough on the stomach. With the paleo diet, digestion often improves after giving up dairy even in people who are otherwise capable of digesting it.

Legumes have been around for a long time but they only became a staple part of the human diet in the past 10,000 years with the advent of agriculture. The primary reason paleo excludes legumes is because they contain high levels of phytic acid. This is an "anti-nutrient" that prevents your body from absorbing the vitamins and minerals it needs.

The Lifestyle

As you have already read, paleo advocates an active lifestyle. It specifically emphasizes doing light activity throughout the day and only doing strenuous workouts 3-5 times per week maximum.

The modern lifestyle is generally pretty sedentary. We drive to work (sitting in a car) then spend the entire day sitting behind a desk only to come home and sit down on the couch to watch

TV. Even those who make an effort to workout will often workout strenuously 30 to 60 minutes out of the day and then immediately return to these sedentary habits.

This puts your body at risk for arthritis, gout, obesity, osteoporosis, Alzheimer's disease, dementia, insomnia and muscle injury.

By rejecting this pattern of being sedentary, paleo helps you to naturally improve your physical health and strengthen both bones and muscle at a steady, safe pace. It also helps strengthen your metabolism by keeping your activity level consistently up. By being more consistently active, you keep your metabolism functioning in high gear all day long because you have increased the number of calories your body needs to burn throughout the day.

Chapter 4: Tips for Making the Transition to

Paleo

At first, it can seem like an impossible challenge to adopt a paleo diet. Giving up grains, dairy, legumes, and processed food might feel like you are giving up everything that you normally eat. One of the main reasons people fail to stick with paleo—or any positive habit for that matter—is that they fail to prepare themselves for the road ahead.

Making any positive change in your life requires the tools necessary to really turn a new diet into a deeply engrained habit. To do that, you have to avoid overcomplicating it. In this chapter, you will learn some tips for making the transition to paleo easier and increasing your chances of successfully maintaining paleo for the long term.

With these simple tricks, you can incorporate the paleo philosophy into your lifestyle in a way that feels almost natural and requires less thought and conscious effort. Of course, the transition will be a little rough at the beginning. But these tips will help you smooth out the bumps in the road more quickly.

Include Protein at Every Meal

Protein is one of the best sources of energy. Next to healthy fats, it's also the best way to keep your body feeling full longer. Make an effort to include a portion of protein-rich food at every meal. That doesn't mean you have to eat a pound of steak with each meal. Keep the portion small and choose a variety of different sources of protein throughout the day.

For example, have eggs in the morning. Then, have fish in the afternoon and end the day with pork or beef. You can also snack on nuts throughout the day. By eating a variety of different sources, you can make sure you are getting a full range of vitamins and minerals along with your protein.

Protein rich foods are deeply satisfying and help reduce cravings between meals. Because protein helps stabilize blood sugar levels, you are less likely to get strong cravings for sugary foods.

It also helps muscle growth which is important for everyone but especially those who are trying to lose weight. The more muscle mass you have, the more fat you will burn. This is because muscle burns more calories to maintain itself than fat does.

So, eating more protein and doing activities that help you build strength are the best ways to speed up weight loss. This doesn't mean you need to become as ripped as a bodybuilder. You just need to tone and firm your muscles.

Make Colorful Meals

Variety is the key to a successful paleo diet. For one, the more variety in your diet, the more nutritious it is. But it also helps prevent you from getting bored.

The color of food can often indicate the nutrition value. Orange, yellow, or red foods are often high in vitamins A and C, for example. Dark green foods, on the other hand, usually contain a lot of minerals as well as vitamin K.

Since there are so many different vitamins and minerals that you need to be eating on a daily basis, it's almost impossible to track each individual one and make sure you are including it in your diet. This is tedious and difficult. When anything becomes tedious and difficult, it is extremely unlikely that you will stick with it for the long term.

So, instead of painstakingly tracking every microgram of a nutrient you are eating, focus on creating colorful meals. The more colorful you plate, the more variety of nutrients you are getting. You can include different color schemes throughout the day and move through the rainbow.

For example, start with deep red and purple berries in the morning and work your way through all the colors throughout the day.

The effort it takes to include lots of colors in each meal is much more manageable than the effort it takes to tediously count vitamins and minerals. So, forget about tracking specific vitamins and just try to eat every color of the rainbow every day.

Drink Smoothies

If you find it difficult to get enough fruits and veggies in your diet, try making smoothies. Smoothies are delicious, quick, and easy to drink. You can pack multiple servings of fruits and veggies into it and just gulp it down on the way to work.

Smoothies are also ideal for those who aren't huge fans of vegetables. You can easily sneak vegetables into your diet by blending them up with your favorite fruits. Richly flavored foods like coconut milk, nut butters, and banana can be used to mask the flavor of the veggies you don't enjoy yet.

This is also the perfect way to make sure you eat breakfast regularly. If you don't have time to actually cook something, just throw some fruits, veggies, and other paleo ingredients into a blender and you're ready to go with a complete, balanced breakfast that you can drink on the move.

You no longer have any excuse to skip your breakfast now! If you're stuck on ideas for smoothies, check out chapter 9 of this book to get you started. But don't be afraid to experiment with those recipes and start making up your own combinations. As long as each ingredient is paleo, you can't go wrong!

Keep a List of Paleo Substitutes

The first couple of weeks are the most difficult. You still have this strong habit of eating dairy, grains and other non-paleo foods so you'll find yourself missing those tastes and textures.

To help you push through these difficult first weeks, keep a list of paleo substitutes for the non-paleo foods you know you'll have the toughest time giving up.

Many people recommend avoiding substitutions and just learning to appreciate the flavors that are available in a paleo diet. While it's true that paleo allows for rich and amazing flavor combinations and thoroughly satisfying meals, it's hard to appreciate this at the beginning when all you can think about is chowing down on a grilled cheese sandwich.

So, at least for the beginning, go ahead and use substitute foods that include all paleo friendly ingredients but may be a bit more processed than would normally be allowed. Then, you can slowly transition away from eating those and no longer being dependent on substitutes.

Here is a quick list of some examples of paleo-friendly substitutes for the most commonly eaten non-paleo foods:

Nut Milks (almond, coconut, etc. but not soy)

Nut Cheeses (coconut, almond, etc. but not soy)

- Coconut Flour (as a substitute all-purpose flour)

- Coconut Aminos (as a substitute for soy sauce)

- Coconut Yogurt

- Almond Butter (as a substitute for peanut butter)

- Shredded Zucchini (as a substitute for spaghetti noodles)

- Kale or Plantain Chips (as a substitute for potato chips)

- Ground Cauliflower (as a substitute for rice)

- Honey or Maple Syrup (as a substitute for sugar)

- Olive, Coconut, or Almond Oil (as a substitute for butter)

As you can see, there are lots of way to substitute many of your current favorites. Soon, you won't even miss the old foods!

Cleanse Your Kitchen of Non-Paleo Foods

The first step you should take when you start the transition to paleo is to purge your kitchen of food that is not paleo friendly. You may not have control over what is offered at a restaurant or a friend's dinner party, but you do have control over the food that is in your own home.

Temptations and cravings are hard enough on their own. You shouldn't make them harder by keeping those tempting foods in your home. The easy access only makes the craving stronger.

Some people assume that success on a diet means facing those temptations as often as possible and resisting them. They assume it is about pure willpower and has nothing to do with proper planning or strategies to help you make it through tough times. However, you wouldn't tell a smoker who is trying to quit to keep cigarettes in the house.

Help yourself by making your home as paleo friendly as possible. There will be days when your willpower is strong and you don't experience a single craving. But there will also be tougher days when all you can think about it is eating a whole batch of cookies. With a paleo friendly home, you can power through these tougher days without breaking your commitment to paleo since there are no cookies—or even ingredients for cookies—in the house.

In addition to purging non-paleo foods, make sure to keep some healthy paleo snacks that you can munch on as an alternative. If you've got a craving for cookies, make some paleo friendly cookies with coconut flour and other paleo substitutes.

Create Meal Plans in Advance

Thorough planning—with a dash of willpower—is the key to success on paleo or any diet. You should be creating weekly meal plans full of paleo friendly recipes. This way, when you go shopping, you can buy exactly the ingredients that you know you will need for the week and nothing else.

With this plan and with a kitchen that contains only those ingredients to carry through with that plan, you'll be able to guarantee that you stick with paleo day in and day out.

Planning out your meals for the week in advance helps take the guesswork out of meal time. You won't have to stand in front of the fridge staring at the food and wondering what to cook. You won't have to worry about not having anything to eat.

It is usually in these unsure moments when you're not sure what to eat that you break your diet and just go for something easy and familiar (and not paleo). By planning, you are saving yourself from this common struggle.

With your meals planned out, you can even go the extra step and cook them all in advance. Then, just store them in meal-sized portions and reheat throughout the week. This is a great strategy for those who are often too tired to cook after work.

Eat Every 3 Hours

Our paleo ancestors did not sit down to 3 square meals a day. They pretty much just ate whenever they found food. This means that our bodies have evolved to digest small portions throughout the day. It's less suited to breaking down one gigantic meal for hours and then having a long, hungry break until the next big, difficult meal.

Help your metabolism and fight cravings by eating smaller portions more frequently. You should try to eat something every 3 hours and avoid gorging yourself at any meal. By eating a small portion every 3 hours, you are giving your metabolism just enough to continue staying in high gear throughout the day. Rather than cycling between turning on and shutting off, more frequent meals will keep it consistently on.

Frequent meals also help prevent cravings. It will keep your blood sugar levels more stabilized so that you don't crash or drop too low before your next meal. It will also save you from hunger pains between meals and make it easier to avoid overeating.

A good trick for this is to break each meal in half. Rather than eat your whole breakfast in the morning, eat half and save the rest for a mid-morning boost. Do the same with lunch and dinner.

In the meal plan you'll find in chapter 5, you will get 3 recipes per day (breakfast, lunch, and dinner). This is for convenience's sake since you probably don't want to cook 6 separate meals for each day. So divide up the portions yourself by making enough of each recipe to have 2 smaller portions of each.

Use Cheat Days

Some people are purists and assume that the only way to succeed on paleo is to cut out all the banned foods 100%. Any cheating is considered a total failure. For some, this is what works best for them. Going cold turkey is their way of managing their cravings.

For others, this strategy doesn't work as well. The stress of going cold turkey can get so overwhelming that they end up just binging on all their favorite taboo foods and feeling too guilty afterword to keep trying paleo. To avoid these binges and lower your overall stress, consider using this cheat day strategy:

When you first start, designate 1 day per week that is your "cheat day." On this day, you can eat non-paleo foods. However, that doesn't mean you should *only* eat non-paleo foods. More importantly, you should not binge on them. Enjoy a couple cookies on your cheat day, yes, you deserve it! But just have a couple and make sure you take your time. Eat them slowly, savor the taste and texture. Then, chase them down with a paleo-friendly smoothie!

After 3-4 weeks, extend the time between cheat days. Include a cheat day every 10 to 14 days. As time goes on and you become more used to your paleo diet, you can keep extending the time between cheat days. You can either do this until you no longer eat these foods at all or just go until you only eat them on rare special occasions like major holidays.

When you find yourself having a craving before your cheat day, you can power through it by reminding yourself that you only have to wait until cheat day to indulge that craving.

Go Paleo with Friends

Multiple studies have shown that people who are trying to make healthy, positive improvements in their lives are much more likely to succeed if they make those improvements with friends. Paleo is no exception to this rule.

It makes sense when you think about it. Try to recall any challenging time in your life. Did you have friends by your side helping you get through it? If not, can you imagine how much better it would have been if you had?

By having a friend—or group of friends—who are all going through this transition with you. You can share your experiences with each other, give each other advice, keep each other motivated, and share tips and recipes with each other.

When you're having a particularly difficult time, you know you can call up your friend and they will understand exactly what you are going through and likely be able to give you some advice or encouragement to push through.

Keep a Progress Journal

One of the best ways to stay on track and stay motivated is to write everything down. Keep track of your progress. Get a notebook for just this purpose.

Start by writing down your goals. Include a clear and precise long term goal and then break that goal down into clear short term goals. By clear, I mean be precise and set exact time frames. For example, rather than saying "I want to lose weight." Say "I want to lose 60 pounds in the next 6 months."

Then break down that 6 month goal into weekly and monthly goals such as losing 2-3 pounds per week or 10 pounds per month.

Once you've written down your goals, write daily entries of your progress. Here are some ideas for things to include in your daily entries:

What did you eat?
How did you feel throughout the day?
How did you feel after each meal?
Did you have any cheat foods? If so, list them.
What was your most difficult moment of the day?
What was your most positive experience of the day?

Chapter 5: Your First 30 Days

Now that you have read through all of the detailed information in this book regarding the paleo diet, you are officially ready to take the plunge and try out your first 30 days on the paleo diet!

Of course, even if you are totally motivated to get started and you have all this new information about how to do it, you can still feel a little bit overwhelmed about making such a major transformation to the way you eat.

Without dairy or grains (not to mention legumes and processed foods), you might be at a total loss as to what you can eat. But don't worry, the paleo diet is far from bland and boring. There are lots of exciting flavors and food combinations you can create using 100% paleo friendly ingredients.

To help make the transition even easier for you, you'll get a full 30 day meal plan complete with paleo meals for every time of the day. In chapters 6 through 9, you'll get the recipes for every single meal in this meal plan. You'll also get a few bonus recipes in case you get inspired to change things up and modify the meal plan.

Don't feel like you have to stick to this exact plan, though. Feel free to add, take away, or rearrange the meals to suit you. You can even get rid of recipes and replace them with a different paleo recipe you want to try. The important thing with this first 30 days is that you stick to the paleo guidelines as closely as possible.

If you decide after those 30 days that strict paleo is not for you, modify to suit your body and your needs. You don't have to work for paleo. Let paleo work for you.

With all that in mind, you may recall from the previous chapter that it is recommended to eat 6 smaller meals throughout the day rather than 3 large meals. You'll notice that this meal plan includes the traditional 3 large meal structure. However, that is simply for ease of cooking. You probably don't have the time or energy to cook 6 separate meals every day. So to keep things simple, just cook a double portion of each meal and split it in two.

For example, eat half of your breakfast when you wake up and save the second half for a mid-morning meal. This way, you aren't spending any more time cooking than you normally would and you're still eating as much as you should be.

So, take a look at this meal plan and either print it out and use it exactly as it is or simply keep it as a source of inspiration as you create your own paleo meal plan for the next 30 days. Whatever you decide, you'll be making the right decision for your own health and you'll be well on your way to experiencing the many benefits of paleo!

Day 1

Breakfast	Lunch	Dinner	Snack
Paleo Granola	Crab-Stuffed Tomatoes with Eggs	Paleo Spaghetti	Paleo Trail Mix

Day 2

Breakfast	Lunch	Dinner	Snack
Paleo Granola	Crab-Stuffed Tomatoes with Eggs	Almond Crusted Chicken Legs	Paleo Trail Mix

Day 3

Breakfast	Lunch	Dinner	Snack
Paleo Granola	Carrot & Sweet Potato Soup	Roast Beef	Paleo Trail Mix

Day 4

Breakfast	Lunch	Dinner	Snack
Paleo Granola	Carrot & Sweet Potato Soup	Pork & Avocado Salad	Paleo Trail Mix

Day 5

Breakfast	Lunch	Dinner	Snack
Paleo Granola	Pesto Salmon & Salad	Paleo Casserole	Paleo Trail Mix

Day 6

Breakfast	Lunch	Dinner	Snack
Paleo Granola	Pesto Salmon & Salad	Hungarian Goulash	Paleo Trail Mix

Day 7

Breakfast	Lunch	Dinner	Snack
Coconut Pancakes	Chicken "Tortilla" Soup	Veggie Salmon Bake	Paleo Trail Mix

Day 8

Breakfast	Lunch	Dinner	Snack
Carrot & Almond Pudding	Crab-Stuffed Tomatoes	Paleo Spaghetti	Cauliflower Popcorn

with Eggs

Day 9

Breakfast	Lunch	Dinner	Snack
Carrot & Almond Pudding	Crab-Stuffed Tomatoes with Eggs	Almond Crusted Chicken Legs	Cauliflower Popcorn

Day 10

Breakfast	Lunch	Dinner	Snack
Carrot & Almond Pudding	Paleo Ceviche	Roast Beef	Cauliflower Popcorn

Day 11

Breakfast	Lunch	Dinner	Snack
Carrot & Almond Pudding	Paleo Ceviche	Paleo Casserole	Cauliflower Popcorn

Day 12

Breakfast	Lunch	Dinner	Snack
Carrot & Almond Pudding	Pesto Salmon & Salad	Pork & Avocado Salad	Cauliflower Popcorn

Day 13

Breakfast	Lunch	Dinner	Snack
Carrot & Pesto	Hungarian	Cauliflower

| Almond Pudding | Salmon & Salad | Goulash | Popcorn |

Day 14

Breakfast	Lunch	Dinner	Snack
Butternut Breakfast Bowl	Chicken "Tortilla" Soup	Veggie Salmon Bake	Cauliflower Popcorn

Day 15

Breakfast	Lunch	Dinner	Snack
Turkey & Pear Sausage	Carrot & Sweet Potato Soup	Paleo Spaghetti	Prosciutto Wrapped Fruit

Day 16

Breakfast	Lunch	Dinner	Snack
Turkey & Pear Sausage	Carrot & Sweet Potato Soup	Almond Crusted Chicken Legs	Prosciutto Wrapped Fruit

Day 17

Breakfast	Lunch	Dinner	Snack
Turkey & Pear Sausage	Paleo Egg Salad	Roast Beef	Prosciutto Wrapped Fruit

Day 18

Breakfast	Lunch	Dinner	Snack
Turkey & Pear Sausage	Paleo Egg Salad	Pork & Avocado Salad	Prosciutto Wrapped Fruit

Day 19

Breakfast	Lunch	Dinner	Snack
Turkey & Pear Sausage	Paleo Ceviche	Paleo Casserole	Prosciutto Wrapped Fruit

Day 20

Breakfast	Lunch	Dinner	Snack
Turkey & Pear Sausage	Paleo Ceviche	Hungarian Goulash	Prosciutto Wrapped Fruit

Day 21

Breakfast	Lunch	Dinner	Snack
Sweet Potato Waffles	Chicken "Tortilla" Soup	Veggie Salmon Bake	Prosciutto Wrapped Fruit

Day 22

Breakfast	Lunch	Dinner	Snack
Plantain & Avocado Bowl	Carrot & Sweet Potato Soup	Paleo Spaghetti	Paleo Energy Bars

Day 23

Breakfast	Lunch	Dinner	Snack
Plantain & Avocado Bowl	Carrot & Sweet Potato Soup	Almond Crusted Chicken Legs	Paleo Energy Bars

Day 24

Breakfast	Lunch	Dinner	Snack
Plantain & Avocado Bowl	Paleo Ceviche	Roast Beef	Paleo Energy Bars

Day 25

Breakfast	Lunch	Dinner	Snack
Plantain & Avocado Bowl	Paleo Ceviche	Pork & Avocado Salad	Paleo Energy Bars

Day 26

Breakfast	Lunch	Dinner	Snack
Plantain & Avocado Bowl	Pesto Salmon & Salad	Paleo Casserole	Paleo Energy Bars

Day 27

Breakfast	Lunch	Dinner	Snack
Plantain & Avocado	Pesto Salmon	Hungarian Goulash	Paleo Energy

Bowl	& Salad		Bars

Day 28

Breakfast	Lunch	Dinner	Snack
Ginger	Chicken	Veggie	Paleo
Carrot	"Tortilla"	Salmon	Energy
Muffins	Soup	Bake	Bars

Day 29

Breakfast	Lunch	Dinner	Snack
Paleo	Crab-	Paleo	Bacon
Granola	Stuffed	Spaghetti	Guacamole
	Tomatoes		Sandwich
	with Eggs		Bites

Day 30

Breakfast	Lunch	Dinner	Snack
Paleo	Crab-	Almond	Bacon
Granola	Stuffed	Crusted	Guacamole
	Tomatoes	Chicken	Sandwich
	with Eggs	Legs	Bites

Some of the recipes included in this meal plan contain allergenic foods like eggs, tree nuts, fish, and shellfish. If you are allergic to any of these foods, don't worry. Those recipes are marked with a star (*) in the following chapters and suggested substitutes for the allergenic ingredients are given at the end of the recipe.

Chapter 6: Paleo Breakfast Recipes

Mushroom Cups Stuffed with Prosciutto & Eggs*
Ingredients
Eggs
Portobello Mushroom Caps
Prosciutto Slices
Thyme
Pepper
Olive Oil
Directions
Preheat your oven to 350°F.
Scrape out the inner part of the mushroom cap to create a little bowl just deep enough to fit an egg.
Liberally brush olive oil over all sides of each mushroom cap. Arrange them on a parchment paper lined baking sheet.
Place a slice of prosciutto inside each cap and tuck it into the corners.
Crack an egg into each cup.
Bake about 5-8 minutes or until the egg is set. Season to taste with thyme and pepper.
*Allergen Alternatives: Tuna or Salmon instead of Egg

Sweet & Savory Sweet Potatoes with Eggs*

Ingredients
2 Sweet Potatoes (halved)
4 Eggs
Olive Oil
Pecans (chopped)
Nutmeg
Cinnamon
Directions
In an oven preheated to 400°F, bake sweet potatoes for about 20 minutes or until softened. Remove and let cool. Reduce oven temperature to 350°F.

Once cooled, remove a scoop of flesh so that there is a cup shape just large enough to fit an egg.

Liberally brush olive oil over all sides of the sweet potato. Arrange on a parchment paper lined baking sheet.

Crack an egg into the scooped out section of each potato.

Bake for 5-8 minutes or until egg is set.

Meanwhile, season the removed flesh with nutmeg and cinnamon. Mix to combine. Garnish with chopped pecans and serve alongside main dish.

*Allergen Alternatives: Omit Pecans, Coconut Yogurt or Almond Milk Cheese instead of Egg

Grain-Free Coconut Pancakes*

Ingredients
½ cup Coconut Flour

½ cup Coconut Milk

4 Eggs (room temperature)

2 Tbsps. Unsweetened Applesauce

Coconut Oil

1 tsp Baking Soda

1 tsp Apple Cider Vinegar

½ tsp Salt

Directions

In a large bowl, combine all of the wet ingredients.

In another bowl, combine your dry ingredients.

Stir the dry ingredients into the wet ingredients.

Heat a pan over medium-high heat. Add 1-2 tablespoons coconut oil. Swirl to coat pan evenly.

Once pan is coated, ladle in a large scoop of pancake batter. Let cook until edges are firm and the top begins to bubble.

Flip over carefully and cook for an additional 1-2 minutes. Remove from heat.

Repeat with the remaining batter.

Serve topped with fruits, coconut yogurt, or maple syrup.

*Allergen Alternatives: 1 Tablespoon Flax Meal + 2 Tablespoons Hot Water for each Egg

Quick Homemade Pear & Turkey Sausage

Ingredients

1 lb. Ground Turkey

1 Pear (cored, chopped)

2 Garlic Cloves (crushed)

1 tsp Freshly Grated Ginger

1 tsp Fresh Sage
1 tsp Fresh Rosemary
1 tsp Salt
1 tsp Pepper
Coconut Oil
Directions
Puree pear in a food processor until smooth.
Pour pear puree into a bowl. Mix in turkey, ginger, garlic, sage, rosemary, salt and pepper.
Use your hands to divide the mixture into 10 small, flat patties. You can also shape them into cylinders if you prefer.
Heat a pan over medium-high heat. Add 1-2 tablespoons of coconut oil. Swirl to coat.
Arrange sausage patties in the pan. Do not let them overlap. You may need to cook them in 2-3 batches.
Cook 6-8 minutes or until lightly browned on all sides. Flip occasionally to cook all sides evenly. Add more oil as necessary.

Creamy Carrot & Almond Pudding*

Ingredients
2 cups Carrots (chopped)
2 Tbsps. Coconut Butter
2 Tbsps. Almond Butter
1 tsp Cinnamon
1 tsp Vanilla Extract
1 tsp Nutmeg
½ tsp Salt
½ tsp Ground Clove

Coconut Oil

Directions

Heat a pan over medium heat. Add carrots and pour in enough water to cover them. Cook about 20 minutes or until softened.

Drain carrots. Puree them in a food processor until smooth.

Add remaining ingredients to the food processor. Pulse until well combined.

Optional: top with sliced almonds and orange zest.

*Allergen Alternatives: Coconut Milk instead of Almond Butter

Sweet Butternut Breakfast Bowls

Ingredients

1 Butternut Squash (halved, seeded)

1 can Coconut Milk

Cinnamon

Coconut Oil

Sliced Fruits (e.g. - strawberries, peaches, etc.)

Directions

Preheat your oven to 350°F.

Liberally brush coconut oil over the flesh of your squash. Arrange them on a parchment paper lined baking dish with the cut side down.

Bake in oven about 1 hour or until softened. Remove and let cool slightly. They should be cool enough to handle but still warm.

Scoop the flesh out and divide it evenly into 2 or 3 bowls (or just scoop it all into 1 bowl and keep it all for yourself!)
Season with cinnamon to taste. Toss to combine.
Top with coconut milk and sliced fruit. Don't mix it together. Let it remain separate as you would with oatmeal or cereal.

Plantain & Avocado Bowl*

Ingredients
½ Avocado
½ Plantain (or Banana)
2 Eggs
½ cup Zucchini (grated)
½ cup Cauliflower (grated)
1 Tbsp. Date Paste
2 Tbsps. Coconut Flour
1 Tbsp. Arrowroot Flour
2 Tbsps. Raisins
1 Tbsp. Pecans (chopped)
1 tsp Vanilla Extract
1 tsp Cinnamon
½ tsp Cream of Tartar
½ tsp Nutmeg
Directions
Puree avocado, plantain, date paste, and vanilla extract in a food processor until smooth.
Add cauliflower and zucchini. Pulse until well blended.

In a bowl, whisk together all of your dry ingredients. Slowly stir the puree mixture into the dry ingredients. Stir until just combined.

Grease a microwave safe bowl with olive or coconut oil. Pour the avocado mixture into it. Cover with a paper towel.

Cook in the microwave for about 4 minutes on high.

*Allergen Alternatives: 1 Tablespoon Flax Meal + 2 Tablespoons Hot Water for each Egg

Sweet Potato Waffles*

Ingredients

1 cup Sweet Potato (cooked, mashed)

½ cup Almond Butter

1 Tbsp. Coconut Flour

3 Eggs (separate whites and yolks)

1 tsp Vanilla Extract

1 tsp Pumpkin Spice

½ tsp Baking Soda

Maple Syrup

Instructions

Preheat waffle iron.

Add egg yolks to a large mixing bowl. Whisk together remaining ingredients (except egg whites and maple syrup) until a thick batter forms.

Beat the egg whites vigorously for about 3-4 minutes or until peaks form.

Whisk the egg whites into the batter until thoroughly blended.

Lightly grease your waffle iron with coconut oil. Pour batter into waffle iron. Cook until golden. Serve with maple syrup or fruits.

*Allergen Alternatives: Pureed Banana or Unsweetened Applesauce instead of Almond Butter

Ginger Carrot Muffins*

Ingredients

2 cups Almond Flour

1 cup Grated Carrot

¾ cup Raisins

½ cup Coconut Oil (melted)

½ cup Maple Syrup (or Honey)

½ cup Unsweetened Shredded Coconut

3 Eggs

2 Tbsps. Fresh Grated Ginger

1 tsp Baking Soda

½ tsp Salt

½ tsp Allspice

½ tsp Powdered Ginger

¼ tsp Powdered Clove

Directions

Preheat your oven to 350°F. Place raisins in a small bowl filled with water. Let soak for 15 minutes. Drain. Set aside.

Meanwhile, in a large bowl, whisk together all dry ingredients.

In a separate bowl, whisk together all the wet ingredients. Stir in grated carrot, fresh ginger and raisins.

Stir the wet ingredients into the dry ingredients. Stir until just combined.

Spoon the batter into paper-lined muffin tins.

Bake 18-20 minutes (if making mini muffins) or 24-26 minutes (if making regular muffins). Let cool before removing from tins.

*Allergen Alternatives: Coconut Flour instead of Almond Flour, 3 Ripe Mashed Bananas instead of 3 Eggs.

Crunchy Paleo Granola*

Ingredients

2 cups Walnuts

2 cups Cashews

1 cup Pumpkin Seeds

1 cup Unsweetened Shredded Coconut

1 cup Dried Cranberries

1 Egg White

3 Tbsps. Coconut Oil

2 Tbsps. Water

1 tsp Vanilla Extract

½ tsp Cinnamon

½ tsp Salt

Directions

Preheat your oven to 300°F.

Add walnuts, cashews, and pumpkin seeds to a food processor. Pulse until chopped. In a bowl, whisk egg white and water until frothy. Whisk in vanilla extract, oil, cinnamon and salt.

Mix chopped nuts and seeds, dried cranberries, and coconut into egg white mixture until evenly coated.

Spread the mixture evenly over a parchment paper lined baking sheet.

Bake 20 to 30 minutes or until golden and crispy. Stir once after 10 minutes. Remove from oven. Let cool 10 minutes.

Use a spatula to remove the granola. Be careful to preserve the natural clusters that have formed. Store in a glass container.

Eat the granola with coconut milk (or yogurt) and fresh fruits.

*Allergen Alternatives: a variety of Seeds instead of Nuts.

Chapter 7: Paleo Lunch Recipes

Crab-Stuffed Tomatoes with Lazy Deviled Eggs*

Ingredients

2-3 Eggs

2-3 Chives

2-3 Slices Prosciutto

1 lb. Crab Meat

2 Scallions (thinly sliced)

2 Tbsps. Parsley

1 Tbsp. Lemon Juice

Paleo Mayonnaise

Tomatoes

Directions

Boil eggs as you prefer them. Remove and let cool in cold water or an ice bath.

Meanwhile, in a bowl, combine crab meat, parsley, lemon juice, scallions, 2 tablespoons of paleo mayonnaise, salt and pepper until mixed.

Cut the top off of each tomato. Hollow out the middles and stuff with the crab mixture.

Peel the cooled eggs and slice each in half lengthways. Spread a layer of paleo mayonnaise across each half. Top with a folded slices of prosciutto. Tie together with a chive.

*Allergen Alternatives: Imitation Crab (made from fish, not soy) instead of Crab and Avocado Halves instead of Eggs

Carrot & Sweet Potato Soup*

Ingredients
2 cups Vegetable or Chicken Stock
2 Sweet Potatoes (chopped)
2 Carrots (chopped)
1 Avocado (stoned, flesh removed, chopped)
1 cup Spinach
½ cup Almonds
3 Dates
½ tsp Salt
Cinnamon & Nutmeg to taste
Olive Oil
Directions
In a blender, mix together all ingredients (except for almonds and olive oil) until smooth. You may need to bake the carrot and potato to soften them before blending if your blender is not able to process them.
Heat a pot over high heat. Add 1-2 tablespoons olive oil. Swirl to coat.
Pour in sweet potato mixture. Let mixture come to a boil, stirring often. Reduce heat and simmer for 5-10 minutes, stirring occasionally.
Top with chopped almonds before serving.
*Allergen Alternatives: Omit Chopped Almonds

Pesto Salmon on a Bed of Salad*

Ingredients

2 cups Fresh Arugula

2-3 Garlic Cloves

¼ cup Walnuts

½ cup Olive Oil

3 cups Spinach

1 cup Shredded Cabbage

2 cups Sprouts

1 cup Chopped Green Beans

1 Grated Carrot

½ cup Pumpkin Seeds

2 Salmon Fillets

Salt & Pepper to taste

Directions

Preheat oven to 350°F.

Pulse together garlic, arugula and walnuts in a food processor until finely chopped.

Slowly add olive oil while the food processor is still going. Blend until a pesto paste mixture forms.

Pour mixture into a bowl. Stir in salt and pepper. Set aside.

Steam the green beans in a double boiler until al dente. Remove from heat. Let cool 3-5 minutes. Chop.

In a new bowl, mix together cabbage, green beans, spinach, sprouts, carrots, and pumpkin seeds. Add 4-5 tablespoons of your pesto mixture. Stir to combine. Let chill in the fridge.

Rub salt and pepper into each salmon fillet. Arrange fillet pieces on a greased baking sheet. Coat the top of each piece with pesto.

Bake in oven for 2-3 minutes. Turn over the fillets and coat the other sides with pesto. Return to oven. Bake an additional 2-3 minutes or until flakey but still pink.

Serve with salad or steamed veggies.

*Allergen Alternatives: Omit Walnuts and Use Chicken or Other Poultry instead of Salmon

Quick & Easy Chicken Soup

Ingredients

6 cups Chicken Broth

1 lb. Boneless, Skinless Chicken Breasts

1 Avocado (stoned, flesh removed, diced)

4 Scallions

1 Garlic Clove (minced)

Salt & Pepper to taste

Sriracha Sauce to taste

Directions

Heat a pot over medium-high heat. Add broth and Sriracha.

Cut chicken into bite-sized chunks. Slice the scallions and separate the white parts from the greens (but reserve both).

When broth starts to simmer, add chicken, garlic, and scallion whites. Bring to a boil, stirring constantly. Once boiling, reduce heat and let simmer 10 minutes.

Salt and pepper to taste. Top with scallion greens before serving.

Perfect Chicken Salad

Ingredients

1 cup Chicken (diced, cooked)

1-2 Artichoke Hearts (chopped, cooked)

½ cup Red Bell Pepper (diced)

2 Scallions (thinly sliced)

1 Tbsp. Fresh Parsley

¼ cup Olive Oil

1/8 cup Fresh Lemon Juice

1/8 cup Balsamic Vinegar

Directions

Mix together the first 5 ingredients in a large bowl.

In another bowl, whisk together balsamic vinegar, lemon juice, and oil until well combined.

Drizzle the balsamic mixture over the salad.

Easy Paleo Ceviche*

Ingredients

1 lb. Shrimp (peeled, tails removed)

1 lb. Fish or Scallops (cubed)

10 Limes

8 Garlic Cloves

1 Habanero or Jalapeno (diced)

1 Red Onion (thinly sliced)

1 Tbsp. Fresh Cilantro

2 Avocados (stoned, flesh removed, diced)

2 Tomatoes (diced)

16 Romaine Lettuce Leaves
Salt & Pepper to taste
Directions
Juice limes into a food processor. Remove any seeds. Add garlic, cilantro, and pepper. Pulse until finely minced.
Toss together fish and shrimp in a bowl. Pour the lime mixture over. Add onions. Refrigerate and let marinate overnight. Stir once or twice while marinating.
Remove and drain most of the juice. You want to leave some to prevent the mixture from drying out. Salt and pepper to taste.
*Allergen Alternatives: Chicken and/or Pork instead of Fish and Shellfish

Easy Paleo Egg Salad*

Ingredients
6 Eggs (boiled, peeled, chopped)
4 Scallions (thinly sliced)
2 Celery Stalks (diced, with leaves)
½ Green Bell Pepper (diced)
½ cup Coconut Oil
½ cup Olive Oil
1 Tbsp. Brown Mustard
2 Egg Yolks
3 tsp Fresh Lemon Juice
1 tsp Ground Mustard Seeds
Salt & Pepper to taste
Directions

In a food processor, blend yolks, 1 teaspoon lemon juice, mustard seed, and yolks until smooth.

Slow the food processor to a slow setting and drip the oil in carefully. If you add too much oil at once, the ingredients will separate.

Once all of the oil has been added, add the remaining 2 teaspoons of lemon juice. Process until well combined. This is your paleo-friendly mayonnaise. You can use it anywhere you would use mayonnaise. In this case, you'll use it for an egg salad.

In a bowl, whisk together brown mustard and about 6 tablespoons of the paleo mayonnaise.

In a separate bowl, toss together boiled eggs and veggies. Pour the mayonnaise mixture over the egg and veggie mixture. Toss or stir to coat. Salt and pepper to taste.

*Allergen Alternatives: Avocado or Tuna instead of Egg.

Chicken & Kale "Tortilla" Soup

Ingredients

1 ½ cups Chicken (diced, cooked)

2 cups Kale Leaves (torn)

1 lb. Canned Diced Tomatoes

2 ½ cups Chicken Stock

1 Onion (diced)

½ Red Pepper (diced)

¼ cup Pickled Jalapenos (diced)

1 Avocado (stoned, flesh removed, sliced)

2 Garlic Cloves (diced)
3 Tbsps. Cilantro
3 Tbsps. Pumpkin Seeds
2 Tbsps. Spring Onion (diced)
1 tsp Ground Cumin
1 tsp Dried Oregano
1 tsp Ground Coriander Seed
Juice and Zest of 1 Lime
Coconut Oil
Salt to taste

Directions

Heat a pot over medium-high heat. Add a tablespoon or so of coconut oil. Swirl to coat.

Add the onion. Cook for 1-2 minutes until softened. Add the red peppers. Cook for 1-2 minutes, stirring constantly.

Add garlic, jalapenos, coriander seed, oregano, cumin powder and another 1-2 tablespoons of oil. Cook and stir for about 30 seconds.

Add the kale, tomatoes, chicken, stock, lime zest and juice. Stir. Salt to taste. You may not need to add salt if your stock is already salty.

Bring the mixture to a boil. Let it boil for 5 minutes. Turn the heat off and let it sit for 2-3 minutes.

Heat a pan over medium heat. Add pumpkin seeds. Cook for 2 minutes or until crispy. Remove from heat.

Divide soup into bowls. Top with fresh cilantro, spring onions, sliced avocado, and the toasted pumpkin seeds.

Ham & Veggie Omelet Rolls*

Ingredients

6 Eggs

2-3 Slices Ham

2 Onions (thinly sliced)

2 carrots (grated)

2 Garlic Cloves (minced)

Coconut Oil

Salt and pepper to taste

Paleo Mayonnaise (optional)

Directions

Preheat your oven to 390°F. Grease a rimmed baking dish and line with parchment paper. Make sure that there is some paper overhanging the sides. Set aside.

Heat a pan over medium-high heat. Add 1-2 tablespoons oil. Swirl to coat.

Add onions and cook 4-5 minutes until softened and lightly golden. Add the carrot. Sprinkle in a little salt. Cook 5 minutes, stirring occasionally.

In a bowl, whisk eggs with a little salt and pepper.

Pour the egg mixture into the prepared baking dish. Spread the carrot and onion mixture over the top.

Place the dish in the oven and immediately reduce the heat to 345°F. Bake for 15 minutes or until egg is set.

Remove from the oven. Pull the omelet out by lifting it up with the parchment paper and placing it onto a cutting board or tray.

Spread the paleo mayonnaise over the top if you are using it. Chop up the ham into bite-sized pieces. Scatter them over the mayonnaise layer. Gently lift one of the parchment paper edges and fold it inward to start rolling the omelet. As you roll the omelet, peel the parchment paper away.

Set the roll with the seam side down and slice into pieces. Serve on its own or on a bed of fresh salad or veggies.

*Allergen Alternatives: 2 ½ cups Almond Flour + 2 ½ cups Almond Milk instead of Eggs.

Prawn Avocado BLT Salad*

Ingredients

10 Prawns (cooked)

2 cups Lettuce (chopped)

3 Strips of Bacon (dice 2)

1 Garlic Clove (minced)

5 Cherry Tomatoes (halved)

¼ Red Bell Pepper (sliced)

½ Avocado (stoned, flesh removed, sliced)

1-2 Tbsps. Spring Onions (diced)

1 Tbsp. Lime (or Lemon) Juice

1 Tbsp. Olive Oil

½ tsp Dijon Mustard

Salt and Pepper to taste

Coconut Oil

Directions

Heat a pan over medium-high heat. Add a tablespoon or so of coconut oil. Swirl to coat.

Fry the bacon in the pan until crispy. Remove from pan and set aside in a bowl. Reserve the drippings in the pan.

Fry the prawns and garlic in the bacon drippings for 1-2 minutes (just until warm).

In a separate bowl, whisk together olive oil, lime juice, mustard, salt and pepper to taste.

In another bowl, toss together bacon, avocado, garlic prawns, tomatoes, bell pepper, lettuce, and spring onions. Drizzle the dressing over the top.

*Allergen Alternatives: Cubed Cod or Chicken instead of Prawns.

Easy Coconut Garlic Shrimp Stir Fry*

Ingredients

1 ½ lbs. Shrimp (peeled, tails on)

¼ cup Cilantro (chopped)

4 Garlic Cloves (minced)

3 Tbsps. Coconut Oil

1 Tbsp. Fish Sauce

1 Tbsp. Coconut Aminos (a paleo substitute for soy sauce)

1 tsp Pepper

Directions

Heat a wok over medium-high heat. Add coconut oil. Swirl to coat. Add garlic. Cook for 2-3 minutes, stirring constantly.

Add shrimp. Cook 4-5 minutes, stirring constantly. Stir in coconut aminos, pepper, and fish sauce. Cook 1-2 minutes.

Remove shrimp. Continue to cook the remaining liquid in the wok over medium-high heat for another 1-2 minutes.

Pour liquid over shrimp. Top with cilantro before serving.

*Allergen Alternatives: Chicken or Pork instead of Shrimp

Almond Crusted Chicken Legs with a Simple

Spinach Salad*

Ingredients
4 Chicken Legs
½ cup Almond Meal
1-2 Eggs
1 tsp Curry Powder
1 tsp Cayenne Pepper
1 tsp Dry Mustard
Basil
Thyme
Balsamic Vinegar
Olive Oil
6-7 cups Spinach
1 cup Strawberries (sliced)
1 cup Almonds (chopped)
Directions
Preheat oven to 350°F. Place spinach in a large bowl and fill with water. Set aside.
In another bowl, whisk together almond meal and all seasonings until blended.
In a separate bowl, whisk eggs with 3 or 4 tablespoons oil until well combined.
Dip each leg into the egg mixture. Then immediately press it into the almond mixture. Turn to coat all sides.
Arrange legs in a greased roasting pan. Roast in the oven for 1 hour or until outside is crunchy and inside is cooked through.

About 5 minutes before the chicken is ready, drain the spinach. Add strawberries and almonds to the spinach. Toss or stir to mix.

In a separate bowl, whisk together 1/3 cup balsamic with 1/3 cup olive oil. Sprinkle in thyme and basil to taste. Drizzle over salad before serving along with the chicken.

*Allergen Alternatives: Flax Meal instead of Almond Meal, 1 Tablespoon Flax Meal + 2 Tablespoons Hot Water for each Egg, Pumpkin Seeds instead of Almonds

The Easiest Roast Beef

Ingredients

4 lbs. Beef Chuck

4 Tomatoes (chopped)

1 Onion (chopped)

2/3 cup Beef Broth (divided)

2 Bay Leaves

3 Tbsps. Fresh Lemon Juice

3 Tbsps. Olive Oil

2 Tbsps. Lard

1 ½ Tbsps. Cider Vinegar

½ tsp Allspice

¼ tsp Nutmeg

Salt & Pepper to taste

Direction

Rub salt into beef.

In a small bowl, combine allspice, pepper and nutmeg. Rub the spice mixture into the beef. Stab it all over with a fork.

In a food processor, combine broth, tomato, onion, and lard until vegetables are chopped. Add oil, vinegar and lemon juice. Pulse until a paste forms.

Place the beef into a large re-sealable bag with the tomato mixture. Press air out of the bag as you seal it. Toss to coat the beef. Refrigerate for at least 8 hours (longer if you can).

Remove the beef. Reserve the marinade.

Heat a pot over medium-high heat. Add lard and cook until melted. Add beef and sear for 2-3 minutes on each side.

Pour the marinade into the pot. Add broth and bay leaves. Stir and bring to a boil. Once boiling, reduce heat and let simmer with the lid on for 2-3 hours or until the meat is tender.

Remove the beef and set aside on a plate in a warm place.

Bring the heat up to medium-high and cook down the marinade until it thickens.

Meanwhile, slice the roast into pieces.

Pour the marinade into a serving dish and serve alongside the roast.

Pork & Avocado Salad*

Ingredients
1 ½ lbs. Boneless Pork Shoulder
2 Avocados (chopped)
2 Apples (chopped)
¼ cup Fresh Basil (chopped)
¼ cup Almonds (chopped)

1-2 Sprigs Fresh Mint (crushed)
1 tsp Thyme
1 tsp Salt
Water
Olive Oil
Fresh Lemon Juice
Directions
Trim away fat from the pork. Make sure to leave some of the fat. Cut into bite-sized chunks.

Arrange pork in a large pan so that it is in a tightly packed single layer on the bottom of the pan. Cover with water and add salt. Place pan over medium-high heat and allow it to come to a boil. Reduce the heat and let it simmer until all the water is cooked away (about 3-4 hours). Stir once in a while.

Continue to cook until the pork browns and becomes crispy. Remove from heat.

Meanwhile, in a bowl, mix together apple, avocado, basil, and almonds. Do this gently to avoid mashing the avocado.

In a separate bowl, whisk together 1/8 cup fresh lemon juice with ¼ cup oil. Stir in the thyme and mint.

When pork is slightly cooled, add it to the avocado mixture. Drizzle the lemon oil mixture over the top.

*Allergen Alternatives: Omit Almonds

Pineapple Chicken Meatballs

Ingredients

1 lb. Ground Chicken

1/3 cup Crushed Pineapple)

¼ cup Red Onion (minced)

2 tsp Onion Powder

1 tsp Salt

½ tsp Pepper

¼ tsp Crushed Red Pepper Flakes

Olive Oil

Directions

Preheat your oven to 350°F. Line a baking sheet with parchment paper.

In a bowl, mix together all over the ingredients (except for the olive oil). Use your hands to mix but be sure not to overwork it.

Divide the mixture and roll into about 12 evenly sized balls. Arrange meatballs on the baking sheet. Drizzle olive oil over them.

Bake in the oven for 15 minutes or until the meat is cooked through completely.

Serve in a marinara sauce over steamed cauliflower or zucchini.

The Ultimate Paleo Casserole

Ingredients

2 ½ lbs. Bacon

3-4 cups Spinach

1 lb. Mushrooms (sliced)

1 Onion (chopped)

2 Garlic Cloves (minced)

2 Tbsps. Lard

Salt & Pepper to taste

Directions

Heat a large casserole dish over medium heat. Add the bacon and cook for 2-3 minutes or until it becomes soft.

Add onion to the casserole dish. Cook 5 minutes. Stir occasionally.

Add in the garlic and cook 1 minute while stirring constantly.

Add in the mushroom and cook for 8 minutes. Stir occasionally.

Add in the spinach and lard. Cook with the lid on for 4 minutes. Stir occasionally.

Salt and pepper to taste before serving.

Veggie Salmon Bake*

Ingredients

4 Salmon Fillets

4 Tbsps. Coconut Oil

4 tsp Dill (chopped)

16 Asparagus Spears

4 Beets (cubed)

Salt & Pepper to taste

Directions

Preheat the oven to 500°F.

Take out four sheets of aluminum foil. Divide the asparagus, beets, and salmon evenly among each sheet of aluminum foil. Layer them in the following order: beets, asparagus, salmon.

Add a tablespoon of coconut oil and a teaspoon of dill to the top of each salmon fillet.

Fold the foil over to cover the salmon and veggies. Fold the sides up and pinch them shut so that the foil completely seals in the contents. No steam should be able to escape.

Place the foil pockets in the oven and bake for 10-15 minutes or until the fish is flakey but still pink.

Salt and pepper to taste.

*Allergen Alternatives: Chicken instead of Salmon

Paleo Spaghetti

Ingredients

1 lb. Beef (high fat content)

¼ cup Bacon (chopped)

2-3 Spaghetti Squashes (or Zucchini)

1 Onion (diced)

3 Garlic Cloves (minced)

3 Carrots (diced)

2 Celery Stalks (diced)

2 cans Whole Tomatoes

2 Tbsps. Tomato Paste

2 Tbsps. Olive Oil

1 Bay Leaf

2 tsp Dried Oregano

Lard

Salt and pepper to taste

Directions

Heat a pot over medium-high heat. Add a few tablespoons of lard. If your beef has a lot of fat already, you can use less.

Cook beef and bacon in the lard for about 5 minutes.

Remove the meat but leave the fat and drippings in the pot.

Add celery, carrots, garlic, onion, and oregano to the drippings. Cook over medium heat until softened.

Add ground beef and bacon back into the pot. Add tomatoes, tomato paste, and bay leaf. Season to taste with salt and pepper.

Bring mixture to a boil. Once boiling, reduce the heat and let simmer for 45 minutes.

Meanwhile, preheat your oven to 350°F.

Halve the spaghetti squash length wise. Remove the seeds.

Arrange the halves cut side down on a baking sheet. Bake 28-35 minutes or until tender but not mushy.

Scrape out the inside of the squash with a fork to from spaghetti like strips. Divide onto plates and top with the beef tomato sauce.

Hungarian Goulash

Ingredients
1 ½ cups Bone Stock
½ lb. Stewing Beef (cubed)
2 Onions (sliced)
1 Bell Pepper (sliced)
1 Garlic Clove (minced)
1 can Chopped Tomatoes
2 Tbsps. Paprika
2 tsp Caraway Seeds
Olive Oil or Lard

Directions

Preheat the oven to 350°F.

Heat a pot over medium-high heat. Add oil (or lard). Swirl to coat.

Add beef and cook until browned. Remove beef.

Add onions to the fat. Cook 2-3 minutes or until softened. Add bell pepper and garlic. Cook 5 minutes or until softened.

Return the beef to the pot. Add the tomatoes, stock, paprika and caraway seeds.

Cover with a lid and place in the oven. Let cook for about 2 hours or until the beef is tender.

Paleo Sloppy Joes

Ingredients

1 lb. Ground Beef (Turkey can also be used)

2 cups Tomato Sauce

1 Bell Pepper (diced)

1 Onion (diced)

3 Celery Stalks (diced)

1 Garlic Clove (minced)

1 tsp Cumin

1 tsp Chili Powder

¼ tsp Cayenne Pepper

¼ tsp Crushed Red Pepper Flakes

Salt and pepper to taste

Coconut Oil

Directions

Heat a pan over medium-high heat. Add coconut oil. Swirl to coat.

Add pepper, onion, and celery. Cook 4-5 minutes or until veggies are softened. Stir often.
Add garlic, cook 2-3 minutes, stirring constantly.
Add beef. Cook until browned all the way through.
Add tomato sauce and the seasonings. Stir until combined.
Reduce heat to medium and cook about 10 minutes or until sauce thickens.
Serve with a side of steamed veggies or wrapped in a large lettuce leaf.

Chapter 9: Paleo Drinks & Snacks Recipes

Tropical Spinach Swirl

Ingredients

2 cups Spinach

1 cup Coconut Milk

½ cup Coconut Yogurt

1 Peach (chopped)

1 Mango (peeled, chopped)

3 Tbsps. Coconut Oil

Chopped Almonds (optional)

Coconut Flakes (optional)

Directions

Place all ingredients (except almonds and coconut flakes) in a blender and blend until smooth. Top with chopped almonds and coconut flakes.

The All-in-One

Ingredients

½ cup Spinach

½ cup Chard

¼ cup Fresh Basil

1 Avocado

1 Frozen Banana

2 Apples

3 Kiwis

½ cup Coconut Cream
2 tsp Vanilla Extract
Honey (optional)
Directions
Place all ingredients in a blender and blend until smooth.

The Refresher*

Ingredients
1 ½ cups Spinach
1 cup Carrots (chopped)
2 Peaches (chopped)
2 Oranges (peeled, separated)
2 Bananas
½ cup Coconut Cream
¼ cup Almond Meal
Directions
Combine all ingredients in a blender and blend until smooth.
*Allergen Alternatives: Pumpkin Seed Flour instead of Almond Flour.

The Energy Booster*

Ingredients
1 cup Kale
1 cup Spinach
1 cup Frozen Mixed Berries
1 Frozen Banana
½ cup Almond Meal
½ cup Almond Butter
½ cup Coconut Milk

Directions

Combine all of the ingredients in a blender and blend until smooth.

*Allergen Alternatives: Pumpkin Seed Flour instead of Almond Meal, Pumpkin Seed Butter instead of Almond Butter.

Creamy Kale-Avocado Blend*

Ingredients

1 cup Kale

1 Avocado (stoned, flesh removed, chopped)

1 cup Pineapple (chopped)

1 Tbsp. Fresh Grated Ginger

1 cup Coconut Cream

¼ cup Almond Meal

1 Tbsp. Honey (optional)

Directions

Place all ingredients in a blender and blend until smooth.

*Allergen Alternatives: Pumpkin Seed Flour instead of Almond Meal.

Prosciutto Wrapped Fruit

Ingredients

Prosciutto Slices

Melon

Apple

Pear

Directions

Simple chop up fruits into bite sized chunks. Slice prosciutto into small pieces (just big enough to wrap around the fruit chunks).

Wrap the prosciutto around the fruit. Use a toothpick to hold it together.

You can use any fruit you like. You can also use ham slices instead of prosciutto.

Paleo Trail Mix

Ingredients

Raw Almonds

Raw Cashews

Raw Macadamia Nuts

Raw Pumpkin Seeds

Raw Sunflower Seeds (hulled)

Dried Apricots

Raisins

Dried Kiwi

Banana Chips

Apple Chips

Coconut Oil

Salt to taste

Honey (optional)

Directions

Preheat oven to 350°F.

Arrange nuts and seeds on a greased baking dish in a single layer. Drizzle over with coconut oil and honey (if using). Sprinkle on salt to taste.

Roast in the oven for a few minutes—just until crispy and roasted. Stir occasionally. Make sure to keep a close eye on them because they can go from done to burned quickly.

Remove from oven. Let cool.

Once cooled, mix nuts and seeds with the dried fruits. Store in a glass jar or in snack bags.

Make sure you use raw, unsalted nuts and seeds. Your dried fruits should also have no added sugars.

Cauliflower Popcorn

Ingredients

1 Head Cauliflower

4 Tbsps. Olive Oil

Salt to taste

Directions

Preheat your oven to 425°F.

Trim the cauliflower. Remove the core and reserve the florets.

In a large bowl, whisk together salt and olive oil. Add the cauliflower pieces. Toss to coat.

Line a baking sheet with parchment paper. Arrange cauliflower pieces on the sheet.

Roast in the oven for 1 hour or until most pieces have become golden brown. Turn them 3 or 4 times while they are roasting.

The browner you let the cauliflower pieces become, the more caramelized they will be. So if you want a sweeter treat, let them get browner. For a salty snack, remove them when they just start to become lightly golden.

Bacon Guacamole Sandwich Bites

Ingredients

Bacon Strips

1-2 Avocados (stoned, flesh removed, diced)

1-2 Tbsps. Fresh Lemon Juice

1-2 Tbsps. Crushed Red Pepper Flakes

Salt to taste

Directions

Heat a pan over medium-high heat. Fry bacon strips until crispy. Remove from heat. Let drain on a paper towel.

In a bowl, combine avocados, lemon juice, and crushed red pepper flakes. Mix until well combined. The avocado should be completely mashed so as to form a paste.

Cut strips crosswise into bite sized pieces. Slather on the avocado mixture. Top with another piece of bacon.

Do this until bacon and avocado mixture is used up.

Paleo Energy Bars

Ingredients

1 cup Nuts (your choice)

1 cup Dried Fruit (your choice)

1 cup Dried Pitted Dates

Directions

To roast the nuts, arrange them on a baking sheet and roast for 10-12 minutes at 350°F until golden and fragrant. Let cool before handling.

Add nuts, dried fruit and dates to a food processor. Pulse until coarsely chopped. Stop to scrape the sides down and stir everything. Pulse again until ingredients clump together in a ball.

Remove from the food processor and place on a piece of plastic wrap or parchment paper. Press the dough down with your hands until it forms a roughly square shape. Cover with another layer of plastic wrap or parchment paper. Chill for one hour or overnight.

Unwrap the mixture and transfer to a cutting board. Cut them into large bars or small squares. Wrap each piece individually and store in the fridge (for 3-4 weeks) or in the freezer.

You can use a lot of different combinations with this recipe. It is always recommended to include the dates for texture and health reasons. Try cherry and almond, cranberry and pecan, cinnamon apple and walnut, or apricot and almond for more variety.

You can also add chia seeds, unsweetened shredded coconut, cocoa powder, nutmeg, or lemon zest to any recipe for added flavor.

Part - 2

The Paleo Diet is one of the most popular diets around.

But many people are still not comfortable with giving it a shot thinking the allowed foods are "exotic," tastes like crap, or are hard to prepare. If you're one of them, this book is good news. In this book, you'll find 30 delicious and un-complicated Paleo Diet recipes that can help you hit the Paleo ground running. And more importantly, these recipes will help you see that not only is the Paleo diet a practical one but also a very tasty one.

So if you're ready, turn the page and let's begin!

Chapter 1: Paleo-Approved Foods

While you'll learn 30 different Paleo diet compliant recipes in this book, I want you to walk away with so much more than just the ability to prepare these 30 recipes but to be able to create your own recipes off the fly. You can do that if you know the foods that are Paleo compliant. These 30 recipes are like memorizing 30 different answers to 30 different algebra problems and knowing the allowed and disallowed foods is like knowing the formulas or general solutions, which will allow you to solve just about any algebraic problem. In this chapter, we'll start with the Paleo allowed foods.

Meats
- Beef
- Chicken
- Lamb
- Pork
- Turkey

Seafood
- Haddock
- Salmon
- Shellfish
- Shrimp
- Trout
- Wild Caught Tuna (when possible)

Eggs (Preferably Omega3 Enriched or Free-Range Eggs)

Vegetables
- Broccoli
- Carrots
- Kale
- Onions
- Peppers
- Tomatoes

Fruits
- Apples
- Avocados
- Bananas
- Blueberries
- Oranges
- Pears
- Strawberries

Tubers
- Regular Potatoes
- Sweet Potatoes
- Turnips
- Yams

Seeds and Nuts
- Almonds
- Hazelnuts
- Macadamia Nuts
- Pumpkin Seeds
- Sunflower Seeds
- Walnuts

Spices and Salts
- Garlic
- Himalayan And Sea Salts
- Rosemary
- Turmeric

Healthy Fats
- Avocado Oil
- Coconut Oil
- Lard
- Olive Oil
- Tallow

Liquids
- Plain Water
- Green Tea
- Pure Black Coffee

Chapter 2: Paleo-Disapproved Foods

Just as important when it comes to eating Paleo are the foods you're not supposed to eat for successful fat loss, more energy and better health. A key principle that should make it much easier for you to determine whether or not you should be consuming a specific type of food item is this: **avoid processed foods**. If it doesn't look anywhere near its original form, that's processed and therefore, avoid it.

Grains
-   Barley
-   Rice
-   Rye
-   Spelt
-   Wheat

High Fructose Corn Syrup and Sugar

Highly Processed Foods
-   Foods Labeled As "Nonfat," "Low-fat," "Diet," Or "Sugar Free"
-   Synthetic Meal Replacement Shakes

Legumes
-   Beans
-   Lentils

Dairy Products, Especially "Low Fat" Versions

Trans Fats, i.e., Hydrogenated or Partially Hydrogenated

Vegetable Based Oils
-   Corn
-   Cottonseed
-   Grape Seed
-   Safflower
-   Soybean Oils
-   Sunflower

Chapter 3: Paleo Breakfast Recipes

Now that you have a general idea of what foods are allowed and disallowed on the Paleo Diet let's hit the ground running with 30 deliciously healthy Paleo compliant recipes, starting with the most important meal of the day; breakfast.

1. Prehistoric Egg Muffins

Ingredients:
- 12 pieces free-range organic eggs;
- 3 cloves garlic, chopped;
- 1/2 cup kale, chopped;
- 1/4 cup cilantro, chopped;
- 1/4 cup fresh basil, chopped;
- 1/4 cup green onion, chopped;
- 1/4 cup tomatoes, chopped;
- Pepper for tasting;
- Salt for tasting; and
- A bit of coconut oil for lining muffin molds.

Directions:
- Preheat your oven to 350 degrees Fahrenheit.
- Line your muffin molds with coconut oil.
- Beat the eggs thoroughly and add salt and pepper to taste.

- Mix the chopped vegetables in and, after thoroughly combining, transfer the mixture into the oil-lined molds.
- Place the molds in the oven and bake for up to 25 minutes.
- Let the muffins cool outside the oven before taking out of the mold and enjoying.

2. Breakfast Omelet Ala Avocado

Ingredients:
- 1 piece avocado;
- 2 tablespoons red onion, minced;
- 4 pieces eggs;
- 4 slices bacon;
- A dash of Tabasco Habanero hot sauce; and
- A tablespoon of fresh cilantro, minced.

Directions:
- Fry the bacon slices until you get your desired level of crispiness. When done, crumble them to bits.
- Cut the avocado in 2 and scoop the flesh out of the pieces. Mash the flesh until you get your desired texture. Mix the onion and cilantro in the mashed avocado, followed by the bacon bits. Mix thoroughly.

‒   Beat the eggs and make omelets from them. Fill the omelets with the avocado mashed mixture. Add some Habanero sauce if you want some spiciness and zing.

3. Morning Eggs Guacamole

Ingredients:
‒   1 piece medium sized hass avocado;
‒   1 pinch of chili powder;
‒   1 tablespoon fresh cilantro, chopped;
‒   1 tablespoon jalapeno, minced;
‒   1 tablespoon tomato, diced;
‒   1 teaspoon red onion, minced;
‒   3 teaspoons lime juice, fresh;
‒   12 pieces large hardboiled eggs, peeled;
‒   Pepper for tasting; and
‒   Salt for tasting.

Directions:
‒   Cut the eggs in half in a horizontal manner. Scoop the yolks out.
‒   Take 2 egg yolks and mash them well with the avocado. Discard the 10 other egg yolks. Mix the salt, pepper, cilantro, jalapeno, red onion and lime juice in and combine thoroughly.
‒   Fold the tomato gently into the mixture.

–   With the mixture, fill out each of the halved eggs' hollows (where the yolks used to be).
–   Sprinkle with some chili powder - if desired - before enjoying.

4. Prehistoric Porridge

Ingredients:
–   1 dash cloves;
–   1 dash nutmeg;
–   1 teaspoon powdered cinnamon;
–   1 teaspoon raw honey;
–   1/2 cup almonds, ground; and
–   3/4 cup coconut cream.

Directions:
–   Melt your coconut cream over medium heat. Mix the almonds and sweetener in and stir cook for about 5 minutes.
–   Throw all the spices and the sweeteners in and adjust the spicy-sweet level by adding more sweeteners, if desired.

5. Paleo Scalleo-Cakes

Ingredients:
-    2 pieces, whole eggs;
-    2 tablespoons coconut oil;
-    8 ounces cauliflower, chopped;
-    1 1/2 ounces of minced onions;
-    1 1/2 ounces of chopped scallions;
-    1/4 cup water; and
-    1/4 teaspoon, salt.

Directions:
-    Cut the cauliflower florets coarsely. Mince them using a food processor or vegetable grater.
-    In 1/4 cup of boiling water, put all the minced cauliflowers, stir quickly, and cover the pan. Turn off the stove's heat and let the cauliflower steam for exactly 10 minutes.
-    When done, drain the water and remove all moisture from the steamed cauliflower florets through a fine mesh. Put them aside when finished.
-    Whisk 2 eggs in a separate bowl. Mix the chopped scallions, onions, and 1/4 teaspoon of salt into the beaten eggs and combine thoroughly.
-    Pour the mixture on a pan with 2 tablespoons of coconut oil over medium heat and fry for about 5 minutes. Spread the mixture evenly using a spatula. Flip the cake after 5 minutes or when golden brown and fry for 3 minutes more or until browned also.
-    Remove from the pan and enjoy!

6. Paleo Broccoli Cakes

Ingredients:
-     1 handful fresh parsley;
-     1 pinch pepper;
-     1 small clove of garlic, diced roughly;
-     1 whole egg;
-     1/2 teaspoon baking powder;
-     1/2 teaspoon salt;
-     2 tablespoons green onion, chopped;
-     2 tablespoons pumpkin seeds;
-     3 tablespoons tapioca flour;
-     6 to 7 pieces medium sized broccoli florets; and
-     Coconut oil for cooking.

Directions:
-     Grind the broccoli, garlic, green onion, and pumpkin seeds into tiny crumbs using a food processor.
-     Throw the egg in and continue processing until everything's well mixed.
-     Throw the tapioca flour and baking powder in and process some more.
-     Heat the coconut oil in a pan placed over medium heat and in it, fry up to 2 tablespoons of the processed mixture for up to 3 minutes per

side. Flatten the mixture slightly to create round cakes.
–   Do the same for all the remaining mixture.

7. Paleo Pesto-Ghetti

Ingredients:
-    1 ½ cup flat leaf parsley, without stems;
-    1 clove garlic;
-    1/3 cup of olive oil;
-    1/3 cup of unsalted and blanched almonds;
-    2 plum tomatoes, chopped;
-    3/4 pound of squash spaghetti noodles; and
-    3/4 teaspoon of salt.

Directions:
-    To prepare the squash spaghetti noodles, pierce the squash with multiple holes and bake in a pre-heated oven from 45 minutes to up to 1 1/2 hours. You'll know that the squash is ready to be spiralized into spaghetti noodles when its outer skin turns soft.
-    Cut the squash in half when done, take out the seeds, and use a spiralizer or a fork to scrape out the flesh into noodles.
-    To prepare your pesto sauce, puree the garlic, salt, and parsley using a blender. Pour the olive oil in a thin flow while the blender continues to run. Then, throw in the almonds and pulse the blender to chop them well.

- Boil salted water in a big pot and in it, cook the squash spaghetti noodles for up to 12 minutes. Drain the squash spaghetti noodles when done but keep 1/2 cup of the salted water in another container for use later on.
- Toss the squash noodles with the pesto sauce, tomatoes, and the remaining salted water from earlier. Enjoy!

8. Paleo Chicken Lime

Ingredients:
- 1 piece bell pepper, diced;
- 1 piece of onion, finely diced;
- 2 pounds chicken, with bones;
- 2 slices of dried lime;
- 2 teaspoons coriander powder;
- 2 teaspoons cumin;
- 2 teaspoons mild paprika;
- 2 teaspoons turmeric;
- 3 cloves garlic, pressed;
- 3 tablespoons of fresh lemon juice;
- 3/4 cup of cilantro;
- Black pepper; and
- Olive oil for drizzling.

Directions:
- Bring your oven to 350 degrees Fahrenheit.

–   In the meantime, break the lime into pieces and boil it in 1 cup of water. Let it set for up to 15 minutes. Prepare the onion, garlic, bell pepper, spices, and herbs while doing so.

–   After letting the lime set for 15 minutes, strain the pieces and cut them into even smaller chunks. Return the lime pieces back into the water in which you boiled and set them and add the spices, bell pepper, lemon juice, herbs, onion, garlic, and another 3/4 cup of water. Ensure all are mixed very well.

–   Throw the chicken in and sprinkle some black pepper. Mix the chicken and all the other ingredients well before pouring everything into a baking dish.

–   Bake the chicken in the preheated oven for 1 hour. Mix the dish every 20 minutes or so. If the mixture becomes excessively dry, put some more water and mix it.

–   When the chicken's golden brown and tender, take it out of the oven. Enjoy with some olive oil drizzled onto it.

9. Paleoghetti

Ingredients:
–   1 large onion, diced;
–   1 piece of bay leaf;

- 1 pound of beef (grass-fed), ground;
- 1 whole spaghetti squash, sliced in half and seeded;
- 1/4 cup of bacon, chopped;
- 2 cans of meaty tomatoes;
- 2 celery sticks, diced;
- 2 tablespoons of lard;
- 2 tablespoons tomato paste;
- 2 teaspoons dried oregano;
- 3 cloves of garlic, minced;
- 3 pieces carrots, diced;
- Parsley for garnishing;
- Pepper for tasting; and
- Salt for tasting.

Directions:
- In lard, cook your ground beef and bacon together. Set aside on a plate when done.
- Over medium heat, sauté the celery, carrots, oregano, garlic, and onion in the same pan that you used to cook the bacon and ground beef until tender.
- Throw the ground beef, bacon, tomatoes, tomato paste, and bay leaf in, taste if salt and pepper if desired, and let the Bolognese sauce simmer for about 45 minutes.
- While the sauce is simmering, bring your oven to 350 degrees Fahrenheit.
- While simmering the sauce and pre-heating your oven, cut your spaghetti squashes in half in a lengthwise manner. Take the seeds out. Place

the halves on a baking sheet with the cut side facing down.
-    Bake in the preheated oven for up to 35 minutes. When done, remove from the oven and use a fork or a spiralizer to scrape the squash halves' flesh to create noodles.
-    Pour generous amounts of the cooked Bolognese sauce on the squash spaghetti noodles and garnish with parsley if desired.

10. Sautéed Mushroom Treat

Ingredients:
-    1 head of broccoli rabe (rapini), trimmed stems;
-    1/2 onion, sliced into thin pieces;
-    1/2 tablespoon of coconut oil;
-    1/4 cup white wine;
-    2 cups shitake mushrooms, sliced;
-    4 cloves of garlic, chopped; and
-    Salt for tasting.

Directions:
-    Boil the rapini for 3 to 4 minutes to blanch it. Drain the rapini completely when done.
-    Sautee the onions in about a quarter tablespoon of coconut oil dashed with salt until

browned and tender over medium high heat. Don't sauté for more than 6 minutes.
-    Throw in the garlic and cook for 3 more minutes.
-    Throw in the remaining coconut oil, mix the wine and shitake mushrooms in, and taste with salt. Bring the heat up to sauté further until you see the mushrooms become brown.
-    Throw the rapini in. Cover the pan and continue cooking until the rapini becomes tender. Then, simmer with cover for a few minutes more before removing from heat to enjoy.

11. Baked Carrotatoes

Ingredients:
-    1 sweet potato, cut into half inch lengthwise pieces;
-    1 teaspoon of salt;
-    1/2 teaspoon pepper;
-    2 tablespoons dried thyme;
-    2 tablespoons olive oil; and
-    7 carrots, cut into half inch lengthwise pieces.

Directions:
-    Bring your oven to 400 degrees Fahrenheit. While doing so, toss together in a large baking

sheet the carrot pieces, sweet potato pieces, olive oil, salt, pepper, and dried herbs.

–   Place the tossed mixture in the already heated oven and bake for up to 40 minutes or just until both the carrots and sweet potato pieces are browned and crisp. Keep watch every couple of minutes to ensure they don't overcook.

–   Once done, remove from the oven and allow to cool before eating or storing for later eating.

12. A Caveman's Chicken Pasta Lunch

Ingredients:
–   1 pound chicken breast;
–   1 spaghetti squash;
–   1 teaspoon arrowroot powder to thicken recipe if needed;
–   1 teaspoon garlic powder;
–   1/2 cup sundried tomatoes, julienned;
–   1/2 lemon worth of zest and juice;
–   1/4 cup extra virgin olive oil;
–   1/4 cup pine nuts;
–   2 tablespoons coconut oil
–   3 ounces canned black olives, sliced;
–   Basil;
–   Pepper for tasting; and
–   Salt for tasting.

Directions:

- Heat your oven to 375 degrees Fahrenheit. Prepare the ingredients while waiting for your oven to achieve desired heat.

- Cut the spaghetti squash in half in a lengthwise manner and take the seeds out. In a baking sheet with 1/4 inch of water, place the squash halves with the cut sides facing down. Place the baking sheet containing the squash in the preheated oven and bake for up to 1 hour tops. You'll know the squash is good when the skin turns tender.

- Take the baking sheet out of the oven and let the squash cool prior to scraping the flesh off the squash with a spiralizer or fork to create noodles.

- Slice the chicken breasts into small pieces and sprinkle with pepper, salt, and garlic powder for seasoning. Sear the chicken breasts in coconut oil on medium-high heat for several minutes. Reduce the heat and allow the chicken pieces to simmer until cooked through.

- Throw the sundried tomatoes, pine nuts, olives, lemon zest and juice, and arrow root powder in and mix with the chicken in the pan. Let the mixture simmer for up to 2 minutes more to let the mixture become thick.

- Remove from heat, pour in the olive oil and combine well. Pour the mixture on the spaghetti squash noodles and garnish with basil if desired before enjoying.

13. China Chicken Treat

Ingredients:

- 1 cup of chopped onions;
- 1 teaspoon of curry powder;
- 1 teaspoon of dried cilantro;
- 1 teaspoon of ground turmeric;
- 1/2 cup of sliced jalapenos;
- 2 cups of cut red pepper;
- 2 teaspoons of ginger root;
- 5 cups of shredded cabbage;
- 5 teaspoons of coconut oil;
- 6 cloves of garlic; and
- 8 ounces of skinless chicken breast fillets.

Directions:

- Cook your chicken, onions, jalapenos, and spices in some water until the chicken is completely cooked.
- Put some more water and continue cooking for 3 more minutes.
- In a separate pan with coconut oil, cook the cabbage and red peppers until they become soft.
- Split the cabbage equally between two plates and top each plate with the cooked chicken to enjoy.

14. Paleotallian Eggs

Ingredients:
- 1 1/2 cup of chopped kale;
- 1 teaspoon of Balsamic vinaigrette;
- 1/2 cup of cherry tomatoes;
- 1/2 teaspoon of coconut oil;
- 1/4 avocado;
- 1/4 teaspoon of minced rosemary; and
- 4 free-range eggs.

Directions:
- Melt the oil in a pan over medium heat. Mix 3 tablespoons of water in together with the kale, cherry tomatoes, and rosemary. Make sure all's coated with the oil so stir everything well. Cook up to 4 minutes with a lid. Stir once every minute and a half.
- When you're done cooking the mixture, use a spatula to press down the tomatoes so that their wonderful juices can be released into the mixture.
- Brush aside the cooked vegetable mixture and in the same pan, cook the eggs in together with a pinch of pepper. As the eggs are close to becoming cooked, fold in the vegetable (tomatoes and kale) mixture you brushed aside and cook for up to 2 minutes more.

-    When you're finished, splash a teaspoon of balsamic vinaigrette over the cooked egg-tomato-kale and garnish with avocado to enjoy.

15. Prehistoric Burger

Ingredients:
-    1 pound of ground grass-fed beef;
-    1 teaspoon of minced garlic;
-    2 tablespoons of almond meal;
-    2 teaspoons of basil;
-    3 sun dried tomatoes cut into very small bits.
-    5 eggs;

Directions:
-    Combine the almond meal, basil, 1 egg, garlic, and sundried tomatoes well. From the resulting mixture, create 2 burger patties.
-    Cook the patties for up to 5 minutes per side or until you achieve your preferred level of doneness. As soon as they're cooked, place them on a plate.
-    Fry the remaining eggs one at a time and top the burger patties with them.

16. Paleo Pot Roast

Ingredients:
-    1 1/2 tablespoons of cider vinegar;
-    1 medium-sized onion;
-    1/2 teaspoon of Allspice;
-    1/2 teaspoon of black pepper;
-    1/4 teaspoon of ground nutmeg;
-    2 bay leaves;
-    2 tablespoons of lard;
-    2/3 cup of beef broth;
-    3 tablespoons of lemon juice;
-    3 tablespoons of olive oil;
-    4 medium-sized tomatoes; and
-    4 pounds of grass-fed beef chuck.

Directions:
-    Combine the allspice, nutmeg, and pepper very well. Rub the resulting mixture all over the roast on all sides. To help the roast absorb the mixture much better, use a fork to poke the roast with holes on all sides.
-    Core your tomatoes and once you're done, cut them into chunks. Put them in a blender.
-    Peel the onion and cut into small pieces. Place it in the blender together with the tomato chunks and pulse until everything's chopped.

-    Pour in the olive oil, lemon juice, and vinegar. Blend some more until the mixture achieves a thin consistency.

-    Put the roast in a Ziploc bag and pour the tomato-onion blended mixture in the bag. Zip the bag and put it in the fridge for at least 8 hours to marinate the roast.

-    After you've marinated the roast for at least 8 hours, sear both sides of the roast and melt the lard in a Dutch oven set on medium-high heat. Save the roast's marinade for later.

-    When the roast has been seared and the lard has melted, mix the reserved marinade, the beef broth, and the bay leaves in. As the mixture starts to boil, lower the heat so that it will come down to a simmer. Let the roast and the mixture continue simmering for 3 hours - with cover - or until you achieve your roast's preferred tenderness.

-    Take the roast out of the Dutch oven and transfer it onto a plate. Increase the heat of the Dutch oven again to help the juice inside it achieve a thick consistency, which you can use as a gravy or sauce to be poured over the roast before eating.

17. Stone Age Beef Shabu Shabu

Ingredients:
-    1 large pot of bone broth;
-    1/2 pound of thinly sliced shabu-shabu beef;
-    Spinach leaves; and
-    Tamari sauce for serving, gluten free.

Directions:
-    Boil the beef and the vegetables in the broth until you see the meat turn dark red or brown.
-    When done, enjoy with some tamari sauce.

18. Stone Age Sheep

Ingredients:
-    1 cup of sulphite-free red wine;
-    1 pound of lamb steaks;
-    1 tablespoon of freshly cracked pepper;
-    1/4 cup of Balsamic vinegar;
-    2 fresh organic rosemary sprigs rosemary, leaves removed; and
-    3 tablespoons of extra virgin olive oil.

Directions:
-    Wash the steaks. When done, put them inside a 3-inch deep dish.
-    Prepare the lamb steaks' marinade by mixing together very well all the remaining ingredients.

Marinate the lamb in this mixture for up to 2 days.
–   After marinating, grill the steaks for up to 12 minutes on low heat per side or until your desired doneness level's been achieved. Baste the steaks with the marinade while grilling.

19. Drunk Chicken

Ingredients:
–   1 clove garlic;
–   1 cup of organic Marsala wine;
–   1 sweet onion sliced thinly;
–   2 cups of rinsed and sliced Portobello mushrooms;
–   2 sprigs of fresh rosemary, stems removed;
–   2 tablespoons of red wine vinegar;
–   4 Free range organic chicken breast fillets;
–   4 tablespoons of extra virgin olive oil; and
–   Freshly cracked pepper for tasting.

Directions:
–   Bring the oven to 375 degrees Fahrenheit.
–   Put the chicken breasts inside a baking dish. Use the mushrooms to cover the breast fillets.
–   Combine the red wine, red wine vinegar, 3 tablespoons of extra-virgin olive oil, and rosemary.

-    Sautee the onion and garlic in 1 tablespoon of extra-virgin olive oil until tender. When cooked, spread over the mushrooms and chicken breast fillets in the baking dish.

-    Pour the red wine mixture on the chicken fillets and bake in the heated oven for up to 45 minutes or until your desired level of doneness is achieved.

20. Paleo Shrimpepper

Ingredients:
-    1 1/2 pounds of peeled, raw shrimps;
-    1 tablespoon of coconut aminos;
-    1 tablespoon of fish sauce;
-    1 teaspoon of black pepper;
-    1/4 cup of fresh cilantro;
-    3 tablespoons of coconut oil; and
-    4 cloves of garlic.

Directions:

-    Melt the coconut oil in low heat. Sautee the garlic in it for 3 minutes with frequent stirring. Don't let the garlic turn brown.

-    Throw the shrimps in and sauté until they turn pink or approximately 5 minutes. Mix the fish sauce, pepper, and coconut aminos in and continue sautéing for another 2 minutes.

\-   Transfer the shrimps on a serving plate. Increase the heat under the pan to heat the liquid aminos further for up to 2 additional minutes.

\-   Pour the liquids in the pan onto the shrimps and top with chopped cilantros to enjoy.

21. Stone Age Strawberry Ice Cream

Ingredients:
-     1 cup of strawberries, frozen and chopped;
-     1 pinch of salt;
-     1 teaspoon of pure and natural vanilla extract;
-     1/2 heaping cup of sunflower seed butter;
-     2 cups of coconut milk (full fat);
-     2 pieces of egg yolk; and
-     3/4 cup of homemade strawberry sauce.

For The Homemade Strawberry Sauce:
-     1 teaspoon of lemon juice;
-     1/2 cup (packed) of dates; and
-     3 cups strawberries, frozen.

Directions:
-     For the strawberry sauce, place the dates, strawberries, and lemon juice in a small pan placed over medium heat. Cook until the strawberries turn soft and its juices have been extracted. If the mixture starts to boil at any point, bring the heat down to stop the boiling.
-     Pour the mixture in a blender when done. Blend the mixture until everything turns into one smooth consistency mixture. Allow the mixture

to cool before you pour it into a glass container for complete cooling inside the fridge.

- Once cooled, blend the strawberry sauce, salt, coconut milk, vanilla, and the egg yolks until once again, you arrive at a very smooth consistency mixture.
- Pour the blended mixture inside an ice cream making machine and churn according to the machine manufacturer's instructions.
- When the churning is almost over and the ice cream has turned thick, mix in the chopped strawberries.
- In a metal bowl over a pot of boiling water, place the sunflower seed butter to warm. Ensure the butter turns smooth before setting aside to cool at room temperature.
- When the ice cream machine finishes churning, bring out the ice cream container. Pour a layer of the ice cream at the bottom of the container.
- Drizzle the first layer with sunflower seed butter.
- Pour another layer of the homemade ice cream in the container and drizzle again with sunflower seed butter. Repeat until all have been used up. Make sure the last layer is all ice cream.
- Use a butter knife to mix the ice cream in the container before putting the container in the freezer for 2 hours.

-     Before enjoying, let the ice cream sit outside
the freezer for 10 minutes before scooping
away and devouring the treat.

22. Neanderthal Fruit Salad

Ingredients:
-     1/2 cup of blackberries;
-     1/2 cup of blueberries;
-     1/2 cup of grapes, cut in half;
-     1/2 cup of kiwi, peeled and quartered;
-      1/2 cup of pineapples, sliced into ½ inch
pieces;
-     1/2 cup of strawberries, quartered; and
-     1/2 cup of watermelon, diced.

Directions:

-     Just mix everything! Then enjoy!

23. Banana Honey Fry

Ingredients:
-     1 piece of banana, cut;
-     1 tablespoon of pure, raw honey;
-     Cinnamon powder; and

-   Coconut oil.

Directions:
-   Lightly coat a skillet with coconut oil. Place it over medium heat and cook the banana pieces in it for up to 2 minutes per side.
-   Mix together 1 tablespoon of raw, pure honey and 1 tablespoon of water while the banana pieces are cooking. Make sure the mixture's whisked very well.
-   After you're done cooking the bananas, take the skillet away from heat and slather the banana pieces with the honey mixture.
-   Sprinkle with a little bit of cinnamon powder after the bananas have cooled down to enjoy.

24. Stone Age Choco Poms

Ingredients:
-   1/2 cup of semisweet chocolate chips, melted; and
-   1 1/4 cup of pomegranate seeds.

Directions:
-   Use liners to line a small muffin tin. Put 2 teaspoons of melted chocolate in each of the muffin tin's cups. Pepper the top of the choco-filled cups with pomegranate seeds before using more melted choco to drizzle each cup.

- Place the muffin tin in the fridge for about 20 minutes or until firm.

25. Paleo Choco Berry Cubes

Ingredients:
- 2 cups of chocolate chips;
- 2 tablespoons of coconut oil; and
- 16 pieces fresh strawberries, including stems.

Directions:
- Mix together well the coconut oil and melted choco chips in a medium-sized bowl.
- At the bottom of each ice cube mold, layer a spoonful of the chocolate mixture.
- Top each of the chocolate layered cube with a strawberry, with the stems protruding upward.
- With the remaining melted chocolate mixture, fill up all the strawberry and chocolate filled molds.
- Leave in the freezer for up to 5 hours to solidify the chocolate before enjoying.

26. Popped Cauliflowers

Ingredients:
-    1/2 head of cauliflower, diced small like popcorn;
-    1/2 teaspoon of dried chives;
-    1/2 teaspoon of onion powder;
-    Extra virgin olive oil; and
-    Salt.

Directions:
-    Bring your oven to 450 degrees Fahrenheit.
-    In olive oil, toss the cauliflower pieces.
-    Drizzle salt over the olive oil-tossed cauliflower then spread on a parchment paper lined baking sheet.
-    Bake in the pre-heated oven for 30 minutes. In between, turn the cauliflower twice.
-    Remove from the oven and drizzle with chives and onion powder to enjoy.

27. Cantaloupe Prosciutto Wraps

Ingredients:

- 1 tablespoon of fresh chopped mint leaves;
- 1/2 cantaloupe;
- 1/3 cup of balsamic vinegar;
- 2 teaspoons of extra virgin olive oil;
- 3 ounces of sliced prosciutto; and
- Fresh ground black pepper.

Directions:
- Cut the cantaloupe into 6 wedges before further cutting into 1.5-inch pieces. Remove the rinds.
- Cut the prosciutto into strips that are 1 1/4 x 3 1/2 in size. Use the prosciutto strips to wrap each of the cantaloupe pieces, and use a toothpick to secure the wrap.
- Prepare the balsamic glaze by heating the balsamic vinegar on a small-sized skillet placed over medium-high heat. Let the vinegar simmer for 3 to 4 minutes or just until you see the vinegar start to become thick and shrink in volume to about 1 tablespoon only.
- Drizzle olive oil and the balsamic glaze on a serving plate. Put the wraps on the plate and drizzle with pepper and mint to enjoy.

28. Paleomus (Paleo Hummus)

Ingredients:

-    1 head of cauliflower, cut into smaller florets;
-    4 tablespoons of tahini;
-    4 tablespoons of olive oil for the hummus;
-    1 tablespoon of olive oil for roasting the vegetables;
-    4 tablespoons of lemon juice;
-    1 teaspoon of salt;
-    1 teaspoon of garlic powder;
-    1/2 of a red pepper, sliced;
-    1/2 of an eggplant, sliced;
-    1/2 teaspoon of cumin;
-    1/4 teaspoon of black pepper;
-    Paprika for garnish; and
-    Olive oil for garnish.

Directions:
-    Bring your oven to 400 degrees Fahrenheit.
-    Use aluminum foil to cover a cookie sheet. Pour a tablespoon of the olive oil on the cookie sheet and evenly spread it out over the sheet.
-    Place the cut up red peppers, eggplant, and cauliflower florets on the sheet and bake the vegetables in the oven for up to 40 minutes, flipping them at the midpoint of the bake.
-    When done, bring out the vegetables from the oven and let them cool.
-    Put the grilled vegetables, 4 tablespoons of olive oil, tahini, garlic powder, salt, lemon juice, pepper, and cumin in a blender and blend until you get a hummus-like texture.

– Garnish the humus with olive oil and paprika when done.

29. Asparagus Prosciutto Wraps

Ingredients:
- 1 bunch of asparagus;
- 1/4 pound of prosciutto;
- Pepper, to taste; and
- Optional olive oil.

Directions:
- Heat your oven to 350 degrees Fahrenheit.
- Boil the asparagus in water for 2 minutes.
- Immediately take the asparagus out of the boiling water after 2 minutes and put it in a bowl of water and ice.
- After being cooled down, take 23 asparagus spears and wrap with prosciutto. Line them up on a baking sheet and drizzle with pepper and - if desired - olive oil.
- Bake in the oven for 7 minutes or until crispy.

30. Sweet Rosemary Potatoes

Ingredients:
-   1 teaspoon pepper;
-   1 teaspoon salt;
-   12 tablespoons olive oil;
-   2 medium size sweet potatoes, cut into 1" cubes; and
-   2 sprigs of fresh rosemary, chopped (or 1 tablespoon dried rosemary).

Directions:
-   Heat your oven to 425 degrees Fahrenheit and place the rack in the upper third level. Use parchment paper to line a baking sheet.
-   Mix all the ingredients together in a medium-sized bowl and toss so that the sweet potatoes will be coated with the mixture.
-   Spread the coated sweet potatoes evenly on the baking sheet.
-   Roast in the oven for up to 30 minutes or until the potatoes turn golden brown.

Conclusion

Thanks for buying this book. I hope that more than just learning these 30 very delicious Paleo Diet recipes, you were encouraged to go to the kitchen and give these recipes a try a.s.a.p. These recipes won't mean much if you don't actually prepare and eat them. Only by preparing the dishes in this recipe book and others like it will you be able to experience the delicious health benefits of the Paleo Diet.

You don't have to prepare them all at once. Given there are 30 recipes here, try one recipe per day for one straight month. If it's too overwhelming, try 2 recipes weekly on different days. The important thing is you start cooking the recipes here and experience the Paleo Diet's delicious benefits.

Here's to your delicious health my friend! Cheers!

About the Author.

David Bailor is author of several cookbooks on Paleo diet. He has written research papers on the topic and currently lives in California.